MW01599076

a light
IN THE SHADOW
BASED ON A TRUE SOTRY

BY

ANNA ZERNICKOW

Tate Publishing, LLC

Dedication

A woman is like a tea bag. It's only when she's in hot water that you realize how strong she is. ~Carl Sandburg

For Mom- Without your help, this book would not have been possible. Your strength, faith, love and courage are inspiring. Thanks for living your life with grace.

Table of Contents

Introduction

"When you were born, you were crying and everyone around you was smiling. Live so that when you die, you are smiling and everyone around you is crying."
~anonymous

If we lived well enough to achieve that goal, we'd have lived well enough. The people around you more than likely will be crying because we, as a society, hate finality and fear death. But will I die smiling? Will that be as easy to accomplish? After witnessing my father, Raymond Mitchell, travel through his illness and death, I know it is indeed possible. It is something I want to accomplish as well. It will take a day by day effort to become a better person. I'll have to put forth effort to become a person who grows closer to God in faith. A person who loves everyone, whether I know them, like them, see them everyday, or never see them again.

The experience my family endured during my father's final summer transcended denomination and religion. My siblings and I were raised Catholic. My Mom and Dad taught us to become very faithful people. We observed holy days with more intensity than holidays. I remember praying on our knees together nightly, reading the Bible nightly, and going to church often.

I've struggled with organized religion since becoming an adult. I can look back and know I've been one of the lost sheep at times. There were times I'd convinced myself religion wasn't needed in life. Dad's death brought out the wonderful side of having a strong, common faith. Faith is what we lived on. It not only gave us comfort, it preserved our sanity. I have always believed in God. I will forever more believe in the importance of faith.

I have attended other churches. I've dug through doctrines and realize no matter what church we choose to go to, the relationship we have with God is what's important. I now know Faith is what it's about. Depositing into that BEFORE it's needed is key. Build it throughout life. Lean on it when needed. Help another when life's going well.

This book illustrates one of the most difficult times my family has ever lived through. It was a period of change and growth. We had to lean on one another more than ever before. We came a long way in loving and appreciating one another. The summer of 2003 offered sadness and learning. We had to accept life's lessons much faster than any of us wanted to learn them.

Many people in my world are grieving the loss of my Dad. We miss him terribly. To see his grin and the sparkle in his eyes again would be so comforting. To hear his voice and to be able to listen to his thoughts about things that have transpired in the last two years would ease my unsettledness. Life without him won't ever be the same.

Losing someone beloved is never easy. A soul gets used to the comfort, sight, sounds, and the security of the one you love being near. When that loved one is no longer around for those precious moments, literally everything seems amiss.

Learning about grieving was good for me as I began my life without Dad. I learned a lot while taking the class hospice offers to help people after the loss of someone they love. Although some of it seemed like information everyone should know, during your own period of grieving, it doesn't hurt to be reminded about very basic things. A grieving person doesn't necessarily think clearly about anything.

Grief is an odd thing. No one can control the severity, the duration, or the intensity of it. Even if hundreds of people are grieving over the same loved one, each must grieve separately and in their own way. During grief, the mind perceives something terribly wrong. The images in your head no longer match the images you face in life. The mind seeks to find the familiar. The feelings in your heart desperately desire to find the familiar. Familiar is gone. Grief grips the very heart and soul of everyone, no matter their personality, income level, race, or ethnicity.

Our society today doesn't respect grief. Our lifestyles don't allow it. Demands are made to keep moving, keep working, don't follow your heart. Work demands a quick return. Schedules demand that life move on. People avoid talking about grief. Only a few dare ask about your journey through grief as you work through it. Death, although a natural part of life, is a socially unacceptable topic of conversation. All this is just a façade to convince everyone, especially ourselves that we are above the sadness.

The physiological design of grief is to force us to slow down. It is designed to give the heart time to adjust to the new images of life without that special person. Literally millions of images are captured and held in your mind of life with the one you miss. It takes at the very least a year to gather enough new images of life without that person to even have a day make sense again, let alone be enjoyable.

Throughout life, Dad taught us how to handle death.

He modeled strength when someone died. He clung to the belief in the communion of saints. The loved ones we would grieve weren't gone, just further removed from us for the time being. Dad had a wonderful approach to a death. He also exemplified a wonderful approach to life.

Dad was quite a character, and is the main character in this story. My father was a true patriarch. He led us, gave us focus, and seemingly balanced our massive family for many years. We have a large, fun, rowdy group of people I'm privileged to call my family.

My dad's name was Raymond Mitchell. He grew up in northeast Kansas in a rural community with eight siblings. The Mitchell family is Irish Catholic, and has many of the disadvantages that are notorious to that ethnicity. My grandpa (my Dad's father) suffered from alcoholism. As with all alcoholics, the entire family suffered because of his alcoholism. Dad kept the depressing stories to a minimum, but he painted a picture of life growing up as bleak at best during his dad's drunken days. He learned to be a caretaker early in life, and continued that role his entire time on earth.

My mom's name is Kathleen Broxterman Mitchell. She grew up in northeast Kansas in a rural community with twelve siblings. The Broxterman family is German Catholic. The same disadvantages the Mitchell's are burdened with are also prevalent with the Broxtermans. Mom has shared a few stories that illustrate growing up poor in days gone by. Mom works all the time. She has taken care of details for many, many years and has kept things going through all her days of joy and sadness.

Mom and Dad were married in 1950 and raised a family of six boys and four girls. I'm the ninth of those ten children, and I feel we were blessed to be raised in our family. I've not always felt that way. There have been times I felt being a part of that family, or one of ten children, was a disadvantage. It's funny how times of trouble shed new light on truth. Today, I wouldn't switch places with any other person in the world. Knowing I belong to a family capable of working together, praying together, laughing with one another, and sharing both tears and love, gives me riches far greater than any amount of money, fame or fortune could offer.

Mom and Dad had three sons shortly after they were married. John was born in January of '51, and Wayne in December of the same year. Joe followed in February of '53. Yeah, I hear it. Crazy or just really like kids??? But, we aren't even half done. Diane was born in January of '55 and Marlene in June of '56. Bob was born in July of '57. Steve and Carol were born only a day shy of a year apart in 1960 and 1961 respectively. The clan is rounded out with my youngest brother and me. I was born in 1965 and Vince was born in 1968.

We are all successful in our various careers. We've each taken vows of marriage; some of us cancelled those and have tried again. Most of us have had children, and Mom has 43 grandchildren and 10 great grandchildren. Obviously, we are a very prolific family from generations past to present day.

Our spouses are an integral part of the family. Some of my in-laws are just like brothers and sisters. They've been around as far back as I remember. I witnessed their sadness in our loss, and it was as great as ours. It made me more aware of what marriage really means. They are as much a part of this story as we are. I feared sounding like I was copying the book of Genesis if I started listing who married whom, and which children belonged to which couple. It's one thing to record all that information with God's guidance, but who wants to read it if it isn't from God? I'm hoping the enclosed family tree will be more fitting.

The grandchildren were a HUGE part of Dad's life. He loved each and every one of them. They thought the world of him. His death was tough on them too. Their love was offered in the language of work. They were there to help with anything and everything that needed to be done. They visited Grandma and Grandpa often, and they wanted to stay and be with Grandpa even when it wasn't easy or comfortable. Each knew that the privilege of being with him would cease to be, and they were going to seize any opportunity available.

Other important people who were a part of my father's journey were my mom's sisters, Anna, Sally, and Mary; Mary's husband, Linus; her brother, Charlie; and his wife, Rita. Father Bill Bruning was one of Dad's very best friends. He offered much comfort, and they shared a relationship that was unique and extraordinary.

Chloe, the youngest grandchild at the time of Dad's death was his "littlest" angel. Although she was so very young, she gave him a lot of strength and hope. She is only two years old now. It seems she should be a lot older because of all she went through with our family during the summer of 2003.

The hospice nurses were amazing and wonderful. Dad called them his "heavenly nurses." Our community came through and showed the true colors of love and concern with expressions of sympathy in the way of food, cards, visits and encouragement. During times of sorrow, these are the kinds of people we need to pull us through. I appreciate all of these people and all they were able to provide for my family during our grief. It would be a wonderful thing if all folks who grieve would be provided the same.

This is a story of a man who reached a lot of people. He was wise and wonderful. His story is somewhat inspirational because he was a common man who showed uncommon valor at the end. He faced death with acceptance and used his mortality to evangelize to many who came to visit him. We witnessed what is thought to be unseen. Blessed are those who believe without seeing . . . some of us obviously needed a brief glimpse and a living illustration. This is a story of living true faith.

My dad Raymond Mitchell

Ray & Kay Mitchell

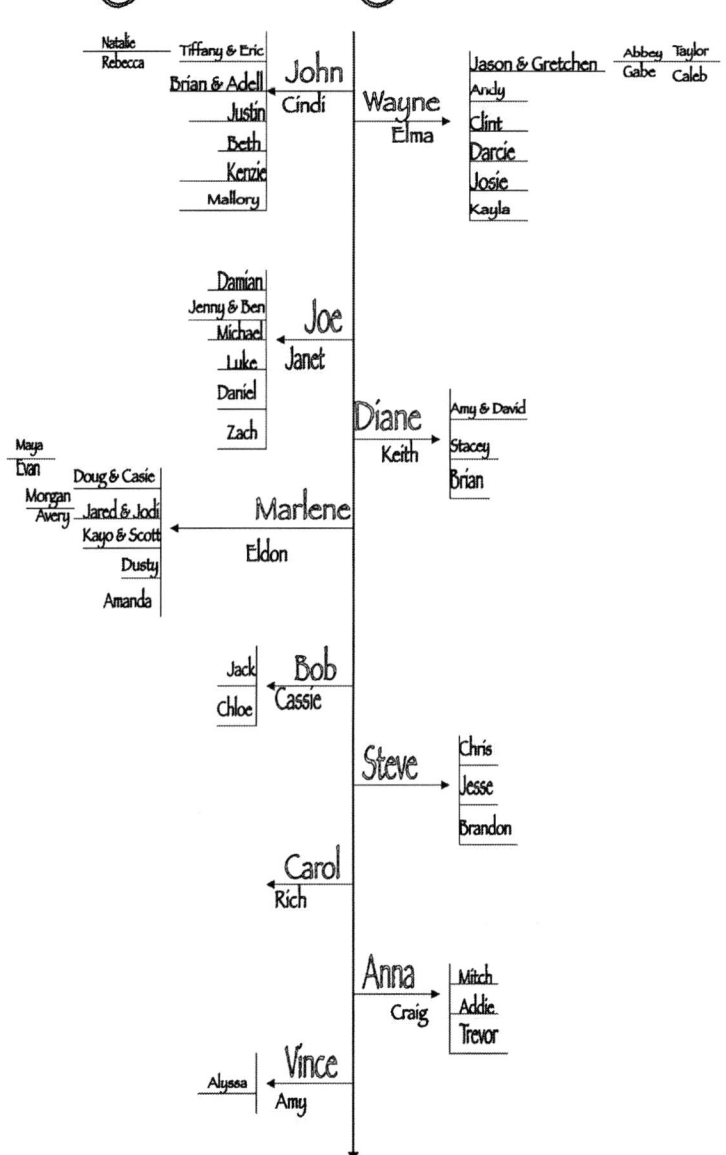

Natalie
Rebecca
Tiffany & Eric
Brian & Adell
Justin
Beth
Kenzie
Mallory

John
Cindi

Wayne
Elma

Jason & Gretchen
Andy
Clint
Darcie
Josie
Kayla

Abbey
Gabe

Taylor
Caleb

Damian
Jenny & Ben
Michael
Luke
Daniel
Zach

Joe
Janet

Diane
Keith

Amy & David
Stacey
Brian

Maya
Evan
Morgan
Avery

Doug & Casie
Jared & Jodi
Kayo & Scott
Dusty
Amanda

Marlene
Eldon

Jack
Chloe

Bob
Cassie

Steve

Chris
Jesse
Brandon

Carol
Rich

Anna
Craig

Mitch
Addie
Trevor

Alyssa

Vince
Amy

Chapter 1

"You wouldn't believe"

On a fairly regular night my husband, Craig, had to awaken me three times because I was weeping so loudly. Upon awakening the following morning, I told him the story of the crazy dream that caused me such heartache.

I dreamed that my dad, whom I had always felt very connected to, had died.

Dad, or "Big Ray," as he was known by many, was a kind, faithful, whimsical, wise and wonderful old man. He was a happy companion to his wife, Kay. They share ten kids (I'm the ninth), 43 grandchildren and 10 great grandchildren.

I used to tell all of my students that my dad was the cutest little old man in the whole world. I even got into the "my dad is better than your dad" contest in my late thirties.

He was a bit of a leprechaun, but his magic had nothing to do with gold and riches of monetary value. Big Ray had known since way before I was born that the magic of life is about laughter and love.

So, in this dream, my family had lost more than a husband, dad, grandpa, great grandpa, uncle, brother, or friend. We were attending the funeral of someone who had led us and taught us, and become somewhat of a hero. I knew three weeks before my father was diagnosed with cancer his death would be huge and leave a void in many people's lives. I also knew that God placed that dream in my heart to accept Dad's illness and death, as Dad himself did. I knew I would have to learn from the experience and look at not the loss, but the gifts received, because Dad was an amazing person. God had been good enough to share him with us for a long time.

The funeral in this dream was similar to funerals I'd attended in recent years. My family surrounded me and there were many friends that we all expected would be there. Among the folks one would normally expect to see at a funeral, I had dreamed of some who had been gone from this world.

Dad's sister, Adrienne, who prior to her death was emaciated by bone cancer, was there in a happy and healthy state. She was laughing and conversing with all of us in the ways that we had all missed for almost twenty years. Another of his sisters, Teresa, had died about ten years before this dream. In life, she had suffered numerous strokes beginning at the age of 19, and suffered progressive paralysis with each stroke. At the funeral, Teresa had full use of all of her facilities and looked beautiful, happy and free to live fully once again. Dad's brothers, Vince and Paul, were there too. They had suffered from alcoholism, but they were there and able to visit and participate, though normally they would need a drink to coax them. Dad's twin, who is non-existent in the "real" world, showed up to speak to us all. He told us not to be sad at the end of Dad's life, but to celebrate his life of seventy-seven years.

As I was growing up, Dad's own role at every funeral was to lift us by reminding all that we were celebrating the life of the loved one and that one's journey to the next world. He would speak to me about not being sad, but rejoice in the fact that our loved one would be with God and no longer have worries that were earthly. Dad also made sure I believed that the loved one was not "gone," but in a different form of presence.

So, Dad's twin, who never revealed his name, came to tell us about the unique status of Dad's existence on earth. This twin came from Ireland and was also one of unique character. This carbon copy of "Big Ray" was just as cute and had that familiar sparkle in his eye as he talked to us. He told us that he and Dad were both UBEs (an UBE-(oob) is a product of a vivid imagination, and a healthy dose of watching the first of the *Lord of the Rings*.) The twin UBEs Dad and the man who showed up at his funeral were bestowed with gifts of spirituality and love. The funeral was a reunion of the living and the dead, and everyone was happy. It was a celebration of the love we had been granted, and the blessings we had so generously been given while Dad was on earth.

At the time of the dream, it all seemed insane. Dad was healthy and had always been a witty, joyful man with a bit of a sparkle in his eye. He was also a kind and gentle spirit. I think all his gifts were amplified in the last year of his life. It was one dream that wasn't wonderful to have come true, because Dad is gone in the earthly sense. However, the entire experience left our family with a sense of Dad's gifts of love and spirituality. He led us through the most difficult challenge any of us had been confronted with in life, and was able to teach and reaffirm our faith, love and belief in God and His plans for us.

This dream left me pondering for some time. Why did I dream this? What did it mean? If you are a dreamer, you know the questions that come rushing forth as you try to figure them out. It is as if your dreams were a jigsaw. Dad's been gone for almost a year and a half and it came to me last night: I was honored with this dream to be fully aware during his illness and death, and to watch with a keen eye, to take in, and learn and grow. I feel like it's important to share Dad's story. He had so much figured out that it will be easy to share. It is my hope that others can be inspired, touched, and learn to have faith and trust again. Or, maybe just know that there are special folks we run into on this journey. Big Ray was one of those special folks.

Chapter 2

"Well, Shucks"

"Out of suffering have emerged the strongest of souls, the most massive characters are seared with scars."
~E. H. Chapin

Growing up on a working farm, I have very few memories of my father ever being sick. He had dealt with melanoma before I was born. He also survived prostrate cancer after I had graduated and moved out on my own. Still, he didn't spend a lot of time down in bed. He dealt with whatever came his way and got back to work. When we were told that Dad was going to have surgery for colon cancer, I think we were all confident that he'd have the surgery, take care of whatever came his way, and be back out on the tractor in no time at all. He did get back to those things . . . just in a whole new way.

Dad had surgery in October of 2002. Only a few of us went to the hospital for the surgery as per Mom and Dad's request. It wouldn't have mattered if we'd have shown up in forces of thousands . . . the news would still have brought us to our knees, in a very literal sense. The doctors told Mom and my siblings that that the cancer had spread to Dad's liver, and there was no way to deal with it surgically. The prognosis wasn't good. No cure. Matter of time. Too many folks have had to hear those words. When you hear them yourself about someone you love, your heart sinks to a new low. It takes every bit of grit you have to continue life with a positive attitude. BUT . . . we do.

Dad did. He was truly amazing. Mom and the others there with Dad that dismal day in October had to play along and talk with Dad about life in general as he was coming out of the anesthesia. They didn't want to share the turn that life was about to take. The doctor told them to allow him to be fully awake and he would talk to Dad at that time. My guess is Dad knew. I'm sure he could read it in Mom's eyes. Fifty-two years of marriage and raising ten kids tends to bond a couple in a way that most of us only dream of.

When the doc gave him the news, Dad looked at Mom and said, "Well, shucks. I thought I'd live longer than that." There was never a bit of anger or bitterness. He had a smile on his face as he expressed his thoughts. The next thing he shared was the need to sell cows to cover expenses and prepare for costs. Dad wasn't thinking of himself, nor of his own future, but of him and Mom. He spent a lot of time in that next ten months thinking of Mom.

Dad had an attitude that helped not only my mother, but all the rest of the family as well. Each and every morning, from the day of his diagnosis until the last days of his life when he had lost the ability to speak, Dad began each day by proclaiming, "This is the day the Lord hath made, let us be glad and rejoice!" He'd follow that up with a bit of Irishness, greeting her with . . ."Top of the mornin' to ya!" He didn't complain and never felt sorry for himself.

The following months were full of ups and downs

for our family, yet Dad remained the rock. He led us on the journey and taught us through the very end. He became even larger than "Big Ray." He became wiser and kinder, more of a teacher, friend and father than at any other time of life. Dad had always been wonderful. He superseded any previous titles and became a hero.

Chapter 3

"This is the day the Lord hath made, let us be glad and rejoice," . . .
~Psalms 118:24

Surgery was over, recovery was fast and Dad seemed too healthy to have been given a prognosis so grim. Mom and Dad were sent to an oncologist to learn of options for Dad. It was a time when the urge to practice silly superstitions took over a rational thought process. Hold your breath, cross your fingers and toes, pray for miracles, and do whatever the mind can think of because you're feeling totally helpless.

There are many advantages to having a large family. There are a few disadvantages as well. One of those disadvantages was we couldn't all go to the doctor's visits with our parents. It might have seemed a bit excessive to have more family show up than fit in the waiting room at the medical center.

Waiting for the members of the clan who were privileged enough to go to the first visit was intense. It was a burning desire to know what there was for hope, and a wish to remain ignorant if the options proved few and minimal.

The report disclosed no cure. Chemotherapy and radiation might prolong life by a mere couple of months. The quality of life would be worse if that path were chosen. There were no guarantees about the quality of life without treatment either. It felt as if we were headed down a path of disparity, no longer able to turn left or right. The field of vision diminished. Planning ahead was out of the question. The old adage "one day at a time" became the only way to proceed.

Ray didn't allow us to believe that the options were ever less than hopeful.

His faith I had witnessed all of my life gained even more intensity. We were looking for a miracle–nothing less. The family prayed. Friends prayed. The priest became an extension of us. My mom and dads' siblings showed support through prayers and fellowship.

My aunt, Sister Anna Marie Broxterman, speaks highly of Dad and Mom's conviction in this decision. "Their decision and the way they lived their lives together until the end was such a witness to marriage. Discussion continued between them throughout the journey. While trying to decide what course of treatment to take, there was clarity in the fact that death was certainly not the worst thing that could happen."

Dad asked his doctor if he believed in the possibility of a miracle. The doctor was a smart man. He answered it wasn't his expertise but he wouldn't rule it out. I was there to witness that conversation. Dad was firm enough in his belief as he asked his questions that no doctor was going to change his mind. Go Dad! No chemotherapy. It made me smile despite the feelings of despair. A miracle was the option Dad and Mom chose.

I am of the belief that everything in life is a miracle, yet I wanted more. Our society is so advanced. Fix him. Help us. No man had an answer. Only God knew the way. Dad was a close personal friend of God, for he seemingly dealt with his illness with more dignity and valor than any movie has ever been able to illustrate.

A few things changed. Mom and Dad were NEVER home. They went visiting relatives and friends often. They went out to eat. It was difficult to catch them at home and as always, they went to every mass offered at church, and all the other events in their church and community. And, they prayed . . . even more than before.

Faith was always a stronghold for our family. For years and years, one of Big Ray's sayings was "the family that prays together, stays together." It was not only a daily practice in our lives. It happened many times a day.

We were praying for a miracle. We were praying for acceptance. The serenity prayer became a mantra. We prayed for the world, for ourselves, and for strength. I privately prayed to be as strong for Dad as he was being for all of us. I prayed that Dad wouldn't have to suffer too much. It was a time that we witnessed the importance of faith in times of crisis. It gave me a sense of the metaphor of faith being like a bank. My folks had made deposits on a more than daily basis. Now they were able to take out and use to their advantage. It gave me a true sense of what God can do. It gave me more faith than any other lesson during life.

It was hard for some of the members of the family to accept the decision that Mom and Dad made about not seeking chemotherapy. Clinging to Dad was the natural reaction. He was the patriarch of our entire family. No one wanted to imagine any holiday, or any day for that matter, without him. The phone companies enjoyed the Mitchells calling one another often to deliberate, even though there was nothing to deliberate. The conclusion was what Dad already knew. Enjoy what was left, hope for the best and pray for a miracle.

Dad led, we followed. Nothing changed in that respect.

"This is the day the Lord hath made, let us be glad and rejoice." It was never said as a more heartfelt prayer as it was by those of us witnessing Dad not only praying those words, but truly living the meaning of them as well.

Chapter 4

"The family that prays together, stays together."

Love knows not its own depth until the hour of separation.
~Kahlil Gibran

Woodcutting day became the favorite holiday celebration of most of the Mitchell clan long ago. Less than a month after Dad's surgery, we found ourselves gathered to celebrate the tradition Dad had started nearly twenty years earlier.

The family Thanksgiving became hard to arrange when many of my siblings began getting married and had in-laws with whom to celebrate. Our family decided to begin celebrating the day after Thanksgiving. It wasn't the typical feast that comes to mind when thinking about the traditional holiday. We gathered together in a pasture, creek bed or another woodland area to cut wood for Mom and Dad. They burned wood for heat in wood stoves to heat the house. As others acquired houses with fireplaces and wood stoves, we cut more. It grew to a massive operation with nearly ninety people and many chainsaws, splitters, trailers and trucks ready to be loaded. After we worked, everyone landed at the farmhouse to eat soup, visit, play some cards and just enjoy being together.

Thanksgiving 2002 was the last woodcutting day we were to be honored with Dad's presence. Everyone showed. All ten kids, spouses, children, grandchildren and a few friends were there to share the day eating, working, and laughing.

Although Dad was still recovering from surgery, he worked like any other time. He carried wood to the trailers, he chopped wood and of course, he had to pick up a maul to show he still had the umpf to split a log or two. We marveled at his strength and energy. We secretly hoped a miracle would be ours to celebrate.

Dad shared that he was feeling well. He had been taking some alternative medicines that were helping with his energy and immunity. He looked good. The sparkle in his eye shone brightly. We witnessed his enthusiasm for life, his faith in God and his joy in being with his family. We all felt so lucky to have Dad in our lives.

The day ended at Mom and Dad's house eating soup, playing cards, laughing and visiting. Dad was unreal at cards. He could bid 7 on an Ace, ten and off-Jack, and would NEVER go set. His laugh was music to my soul. His personality was unlike anyone else I've ever known. Gentle, kind, complimentary, quiet, and personable . . . I couldn't have asked for a better father.

During that year, we knew time was precious. We captured many photographs of Dad knowing the opportunities were limited.

He actually got used to that. Before that final year, his humility would always kick in, and he shied away from cameras.

It was like he knew what we needed. He became

even more selfess than ever before. He handled his illness for himself and made it ok for all of us.

The month after his diagnosis, we were all still abuzz with the "ifs" and "maybes" in which we were hoping. A miracle was possible. We hung on his words, called too much to check on him and breathed a bit more shallowly than ever before. We had seemingly significant conversations that made no difference.

Woodcutting day 2002 was a wonderful day for celebration. The entire family was together. The weather was gorgeous. We made great memories. The pictures we have of that day confirm all those feelings. I'd never known the feeling of walking on eggshells more than those wonderful times. I prayed each time there was a conversation that Dad would still be okay. Looking at the mortality of someone we all loved so much put everything into perspective. Priorities were finally easy to put in order. We all knew that home was where we wanted to be.

It was difficult to maintain our own lives. I wanted to move back in with Mom and Dad and not miss a single second that he had left on earth. I'm sure that my brothers, sisters, nieces and nephews felt the same. I think I can compare it to the feeling of allowing your own child the freedom to go to college. You don't want to let go, but know for the good of all you must. It was time to let go of Dad a little, at least. He had to live each day to the fullest, and I wasn't in that plan every day. I'd be there every time I could be in the plan, but I had to become strong enough to live the life I'd made for myself. I had to grant Dad wings. I just hoped he wasn't ready to fly too far.

Chapter 5

A Massive Mitchell Christmas

Christmas 2002 was spent as most Christmases prior to and since. Our family gathers at somebody's house in mass. We are nearing the 90 people mark, and no matter where we are, we pack in and have a good day. It's one of those perks of a large family. We have a good time when we are together.

John and Cindi hosted Christmas and we all packed in. We ate like kings, visited with one another like best friends, watched the kids open gifts and prepared for the gift exchange.

Gifts are brought for men and for women. We search for something everyone would like. The men's gifts go in one pile, the lady's in another, and we each draw a number. The number one person chooses any gift under the tree. The number two person can steal the opened gift or choose another, and so on. It makes for a rather lively game and takes the stress out of finding the "perfect gift." Everyone goes home relatively happy and a bit less stressed, as the laughter is great for the soul.

There are plenty of smart remarks. Men aaaahhhh in jest at the crafty gifts. Women try to bark like Tim Allen as a man opens a gift that proves to be another tool. There is plenty of laughter in the commentary, stealing of one another's gifts, and sharing in stories of old.

I know we all were wondering the same thing. How many more Christmas celebrations will we share with Dad? I just happened to have the privilege of sitting next to Dad on the fireplace. As I was sitting there, I was fully aware of the short time we had left with him. I felt like there was nowhere in the world I'd rather be than right next to him. His comments were kind and I had a rather difficult time containing all the emotions I was feeling. I wanted to be right there but the imminence of his death and his illness were causing me great heartache. I didn't want to let on that my thinking was so heavy, so I pretended to be lighthearted. I reveled in his every word, his every giggle and every twinkle in his eye.

The gifts were opened, the laughs were shared and we discussed what cause the money we collected was going to for that Christmas. Long ago, we all decided that we all were fortunate enough not to need more gifts. So Mom and Dad didn't get us gifts, and we didn't get them one either. We pooled our money and found a worthy cause to help. It remains one of the best things about Christmas, and makes me proud of my family. It was one of the ways Dad and Mom taught us to "make it count."

The discussion of Dad's illness was now a part of the norm. Mom probably had to relay the information more than she wanted. Consider it one of those disadvantages of having ten children who care. The news at the time was fairly good. The cancer wasn't rapidly progressing. It surprised the doctors. A miracle was still possible. Hope was alive and well, and Christmas cheer was genuine.

The grandkids took the annual picture with Grandma

and Grandpa. All the smiles were full of happiness and pride. I was snapping pictures along with everyone else. Photographs freeze time. I wanted them to STOP time. STOP right there and never move forward. Dad was feeling good. He was happy. Mom and Dad were having a great time, going out more than ever before. They visited friends and relatives laughed, talked, and shared more than before the word cancer had crept back into their lives. Photographs FREEZE time. If only . . .

We ate a bit more, packed things up, hugged and all too soon it was time to go our separate ways . . . again. It got more difficult each time we said goodbye. The whole time Dad was sick, I knew we'd been fortunate to have him as our father for as long as we did. Knowing that did not make it easier to let go, even if it was just for a couple weeks at a time.

In life, there are only a handful of folks we hold so close to our hearts that the mere thought of them being gone invites a host of panic disorders to dwell within us. Honoring those loved ones is the reason we don't allow those disorders to affect us forever. For that reason, honoring Dad, I didn't hug too long, cry too much, kick and scream or find some other way of having an "it's not fair" fit as we parted ways. The family had decided to find reasons to celebrate every possible occasion we could while we had time. I could make it to the next time I was able to see him.

Christmas 2002 transpired much like most Christmas seasons. The major difference was the uneasiness I felt in my heart. Never knowing what was next for Dad was maddening. I worried about what he might have to go through, what Mom would do, and selfishly, what I would do without him . . .

Chapter 6

"Top of the mornin' to ya"

To honor our favorite leprechaun.

St. Patrick's Day was the next event the family decided to celebrate. Dad had always been proud of his Irishness, and we knew he'd be ready to have all of us together again. Although he was a quiet man, he loved the big family galas.

We planned; we invited friends, aunts and uncles; we organized food; we brought Irish party favors. Mom and Dad knew most of the details. We kept one as a surprise. St. Patrick's Day was on a Saturday. Mom and Dad went to church every Saturday and Sunday. We planned on having the entire family show up in church to share in that celebration with them as well.

We arrived at church and spotted Mom. Not too difficult since we've occupied the same pew since I was born. Alarms rang in my ears. LOUD ALARMS. Where was Dad? Not much could prevent either of them attending mass. Mom explained that he wasn't feeling so well and that he was out in the car. Fear struck my heart. Lord, help us. Here we go.

We had been so fortunate. Dad had lived four months relatively symptom free. Missing church with all his kids, grandkids, brothers, sisters, in-laws, friends and community was big. We played it cool. Dad spent most of the service in the car. He tried to come into the church, but would leave in pain shortly after arriving. Helplessness resulted in worried glances cast at one another, hands held tightly, tears fought and hearts aching.

FOR Dad, we went ahead with the party. He tried to join us for dinner but decided to go lay down so he'd feel better for the party. He went to Diane's to rest. Mom and Dad joined the party and did a good job of forging ahead. They celebrated for us, we celebrated for them.

We were proud of being Irish. We are more so now. It's Dad in us. Now, that Irish pride is a celebration upon awakening, as it takes me immediately to Dad.

We put on our Irish green and posed for some great pictures. We laughed with our aunts and uncles. We read Irish quotes and told Irish jokes. Mom and Dad left early. We have great pictures from that party. Looking at them now, I can see the foreshadowing present in the light. I see the love in everyone's eyes. I see the worry, the love, and the pain. Dad had always been the last to leave a party. Dad had never had a reason to miss church. My siblings, our spouses and some of our children remained at the party. We sat in a huge circle and had an insane discussion.

Dad was diagnosed with colon cancer. It progressed from there. The children of someone with colon cancer are strongly encouraged to undergo a colonoscopy. We sat around in our circle of lawn chairs and swapped colonoscopy stories as we had all been through them except for two. They weren't really interested in listening to what they would be going through, but had no choice. Vince didn't share. He's a man of few words and his privacy is guarded. I, on the other hand, was ready to go for a stand up routine.

Looking back, I realize we were desperate to share with one another. We wanted to share something other than the pain of losing Dad. We needed so badly to connect that we found the one thing we all had to deal with and shared, made jokes about and learned more about one another through the stories.

We talked late into the night. Looming large was that Dad was now experiencing symptoms. The miracle? The hope? The lightheartedness? We feigned it now. I think we knew. I know I knew. I felt like I owed Dad. He had been a rock for so long. He was a hero in so many ways to so many people. I wasn't about to be a burden to him now. I would stay strong and deal with whatever came our way.

We prayed that it was just the flu. We knew it wasn't. The next day, Dad said he felt a little better. Whether or not that was true, we'll never know. He acted as if he did. Dad did a lot of things to make it easier for all of us. He remains a saint in my heart. When I complain of a headache, I think of Dad. He didn't complain during the worst of it. Buck up, Anna. There is a constant striving buried deep within me to be more like Big Ray.

On Father's Day, the year after Dad passed away, I heard an excellent message at church. The pastor was talking about being the kind of person in which others could see Jesus. I was busy taking notes and thinking. It was so easy to see Jesus in Dad. If I could become more like Dad, I would become more like Jesus. So my goal was to follow and become more like one great man and our Savior- Dad was still leading me to a better way to live. He will forever be my greatest mentor.

Chapter 7

"Think happy thoughts . . . think of your bride on your wedding day . . . those legs."

It is a considerable accomplishment to be happily married for fifty-three years. A celebration is a certainty no matter the circumstance. Knowing it's probably the last time you'll get to mark this occasion, no one was going to let that day go by without acknowledging it.

We all had fond memories of the 50th celebration on our minds. We'd celebrated in grand fashion with 250 to 300 friends and family present. Mom and Dad laughed, visited many friends, and thoroughly enjoyed the day marking a half a century of marriage. At the time of that celebration, we all fully expect another 20 without incidence. Dad had always kidded that his family had longevity on their side, so he was going to be a pain in the neck to us for a long time. We were celebrating the past and the future, and we were thoroughly enjoying the day. The tradition to dance in celebration was eagerly anticipated. Growing up, watching Mom and Dad dance had always given me a heightened sense of security. They moved over the dance floor in perfect unison and always with smiles on their faces. On their 50th anniversary, it was no different. They danced the polka, the swing, rock and roll, and waltzes. Whatever music was playing, they were dancing. They smiled and looked wonderful. I again had a heightened sense of security. It felt like nothing could come between them.

Fast forward just three short years. A much different celebration was going to take place. By the end of March 2003, Dad had been having difficulty eating. Until that time, he had always loved to eat. Celebrations had always been planned with food as a highlight. Mom is an excellent cook, and Dad loved almost everything in the way of food. Even those things he said he didn't like were often polished off within hours. The foods he liked, such as banana cake with Mom's fabulous frosting, would be hidden on the closet shelf in their room to insure dessert for dinner. He had an amazing appetite, metabolism to match it, and never had a problem with his weight. But going out to eat was becoming torturous. Mom and Dad didn't let us know this. We all just knew that he wasn't feeling too well.

My siblings and our spouses gathered to celebrate their anniversary on April 29th. Dad wasn't feeling well. Although Mom suggested they relax and stay in, Dad had a hunch that something was up, and he willed himself well enough to go enjoy. It was supposed to be a surprise, but Dad was too intuitive by now to be surprised. It was to go like this: Diane and Keith were going to take Mom and Dad out for a quiet dinner to celebrate their anniversary. What Dad suspected was that the rest of us would somehow show up to be a part of the festivities (such a smart man). Most of us were indeed gathered at the predetermined restaurant.

We were all in the party room, cards and cameras ready. Mom and Dad walked in, and we all put on our happy faces. Dad was getting thinner all the time. Mom was tired already. Sadness hung in the air. We pretended not to notice. We took pictures, we ordered drinks, we ate, and we laughed. We all made the best of it. No one escaped the worry. No one escaped the helpless feeling–wanting to do anything to make this all go away, but knowing there was NOTHING anyone could do. We bowed our heads and prayed together.

While we visited after dinner, Dad drew a picture. We kids were amazed. Dad had always been so busy providing for us that none of us had ever seen him draw before. At 76 years of age, he finally had a little time to play. He took the crayons provided and drew a horse and a cowboy on the paper table cloth. We were in awe. Our spouses didn't understand. They couldn't figure out the big fuss over a simple drawing. Mom was laughing and saying that all the time she was raising us and tried to draw for us, we had never been happy with her scratches. Dad draws one picture, and we are all mesmerized. Go figure. She understood. Dad understood. We all knew. We tore that portion of the tablecloth, and Cindi copied the picture for each of us. It was proof that little things really do mean a lot.

Dad didn't eat much, and the party broke up early to get him home to bed. We celebrated as best we could, but worried more than ever. As each couple got in their cars and headed to their respective homes, the conversations were full of questions and thoughts—our spouses try to console, we kids trying to deny. The frightening truth was right in front of us. Dad wasn't going to be around much longer. Each time we were together, the signs and symptoms told us all what we didn't want to know.

The celebration was bittersweet. We all recognized the wonderful relationship Mom and Dad had shared. The commitment they had made fifty-three years earlier was realized and acknowledged by many as a great model. They shared faith, family, laughter, love, prayer, and many dreams.

If they had struggles, they kept them to themselves. We all had witnessed a great marriage. It wasn't perfect. No marriage will be. The secret is to ride the waves. Mom and Dad had been smart enough to ride the waves during the good times and the bad. They had done it. We were the lucky ones. We were privileged enough to witness this commitment to the very end.

Dad put Mom first, especially in those final weeks. He was complimentary to his nurses. The hospice nurses–Amy, Sister Anna, and Mom–all worked for months tending to him. He called them his heavenly nurses and thanked them many times over. Each time he talked about his heavenly nurses though, he would mention the fact that Mom was most important to him and needed to be complimented and recognized.

"Kay, you are first in order here."

In one of Dad's final days, he was told that one of his nieces was going to name her baby after him. If it was a boy, the first name would be Ray. If it were a girl, her middle name would be Ray. Dad was honored by that but asked, "How can we get Kay in there?"

Mom and Dad's love and commitment gave me hope for marriage in general. They'd survived many hard times and loved one another through the worst. Their love, coupled with their faith, made even cancer bearable.

Chapter 8

"Kay, you are first in order here."

Our family had gathered several times with the focus on Dad. It was totally understandable under the circumstances, but with Mother's Day approaching, we sought something unique to give her to show her how much she meant to us. We were also trying to express the gratitude in our hearts we felt for taking care of Dad with her genuine love and constant attention. I offered the idea of building a gazebo for her in the yard at the farm. Mom was not just surprised but almost didn't comprehend what we were offering.

"Why?" was all she could get out as she looked at the picture of a gazebo we had torn from a magazine to insert in her card. We explained that we knew she loved them and it would be a weekend project. We would all come home sometime and work together to build it. Everyone tried to convince her it wasn't too extravagant and she was very deserving. She deserved a whole lot more after raising ten ornery children and being a farmer's wife for 53 years. I wish we could have given her the one thing we all wanted more than anything else–a cure.

Amanda was graduating that day too, so the focus turned to the senior. The day moved on smoothly. I felt like we had maybe found something that Mom could really enjoy. Mom and Amanda felt honored, and the day was fun for all of us.

Dad would often tell Mom, "Kay, you are first in order here." This wasn't a meaningless statement. He loved it when we lavished Mom with the credit and attention she deserved. He wasn't feeling very good but he would never steal any of the light for sympathy or any other reason. He was with us in our quest to show Mom we thought she was wonderful.

I'm sure Amanda felt fortunate to have Grandpa Ray attend her celebration. As ill as he was by May, I'm sure he found a way to let her know how proud he was of her. There was something about Dad. He was able to make each of his children and grandchildren feel they were very special and one of his favorites.

As far as I knew, the day had gone fine. The gazebo was a go, and we had succeeded in finding a gift for Mom to show her our appreciation for all she had done and would continue to do as our wonderful mother. As far as I knew. . . .

Chapter 9

"I'm ready to make a difference, anybody with me?"

There were a couple of things I did that even in retrospect, I think, well done! Perhaps that doesn't sound like a big deal, but if you knew me personally, you'd change your mind. I fight the demons of self doubt and second guessing more often than not. I had a heightened sense of awareness during the time period when Dad was ill and we were faced with his mortality. It was as if I was moving through time with more awareness than usual. It felt bigger. It felt like I was really supposed to pay attention and take notice. Sometimes the gifts we are given are difficult. My intuition and "feeling" nature were gifts during this difficult time, because I treasured every moment with my family and knew, gut level KNEW, that Dad needed to be honored while we had time. No more worrying if I was the cheesy one. It just was gonna' be!

I taught Journalism at Abilene High School in Abilene, KS for a period of four years. I was out of my comfort zone for a while. My degree is in elementary education, but the only position open when I relocated was a journalism position. I love language, writing and kids of all ages, so I decided I could do this assignment. I loved almost every aspect of the job. However, I'm a soft-hearted fool and any criticism was too much. For that reason, and some certification woes, it was a short-lived assignment.

There are many things I look back on from that time and feel pride. The editorial I wrote for my father is among them. I needed to express myself in a forum more than a card, more than an "I love you, Dad." I am an almost overly expressive woman. I'm into poetry, letters, conversations where I push the edges about feelings, etc. I emote on a regular basis. I fear I will explode if I don't get all the feelings out. So, the paper was my outlet to express my feelings about my father. The kids appreciated it. I received lots of hugs, and it was the springboard for many conversations about death, dying, faith and love with my students. It was well received by my mom and my family. Mom copied it and handed it to my family.

It is difficult to fully express your feelings to a loved one, even more so when death is imminent. This editorial illustrates my need to show affection and pride in Dad. It ran in the May 2003 edition of the *Booster*, Abilene High School's student newspaper. It was my small way of trying to make a difference for myself, my Dad, my family or my students. Whatever the case was, it was something I had to do.

EDITORIAL

Raymond Mitchell, a seventy-six year old farmer from Frankfort, KS, is a kind, faithful, whimsical, wise and wonderful old man. He is the father of ten kids (I'm the ninth), grandfather of thirty-four and great grandfather of four. I tell everyone I know that my Dad is the "cutest little old man in the whole world." He is a bit of a leprechaun, but his magic has nothing to do with gold. Dad has known since before I was born that the magic of life is about laughter and love.

Students who know me understand my connection to my father. He is discussed in my classroom often and always with highest regard. Mr. Roth and I have even had a "my dad is better than your dad" email exchange, in which both of us revealed the status of our fathers as the best the world has to offer. Dads are irreplaceable, and facing the future with the impending loss is very difficult.

My mom has shared that every day since Dad has known he has cancer, he begins the day by proclaiming, "This is the day the Lord hath made, let us be glad and rejoice!" It inspires me to be witness to his depth and ability to grab each and every day and make the most of it, now more than ever before.

In thirty-seven years, Dad has taught me more than I'm able to write down on paper. He serves as my life-long role model, teacher, friend, supporter and guide. Since his diagnosis, Dad has superseded these roles and stepped up to the status of hero. Facing an illness with as much spunk and spirit as he, I want to give him some kind of an achievement award.

I propose we stop giving achievement awards to bogus people like actors and actresses. Instead, I say we should award them to what we accept as "common" people on the road of life. Actors and actresses may have more in the line of materialism, fame and fortune, yet they have nothing on the common people like my Dad. Family, friends, faith, and feeling good about what you contribute to this world are much more respectable and satisfying than any amount of fame and fortune.

For the first ever common achievement award, I will

give my Dad an award to honor his character. The development of his character continues even though he is in his golden years. He accepts change with grace, faces each day with appreciation, finds humor in most situations and is able to continue to teach and give to his family while facing his own mortality.

Dad is just one of millions of common people who deserve an achievement award for one reason or another. Expressing our awe in those we love most seems to be a lesson often learned too late. I'd encourage you to start now. You know someone deserving of such an award. Let them know. Give a shout out to your own heroes. You can bet I'm sending this article to my Dad!

Chapter 10

"Too many chiefs and not enough Indians."

The week after the celebration for Mom and Amanda, Mom and Dad discussed the hard facts of life . . . and death. The gazebo wasn't a bad idea, but they knew that Mom didn't want to live on the farm alone. Why build the gazebo on the farm if she weren't going to get to enjoy it?

Discussions about moving to town had occurred for years, but Dad was a life-long farmer, so they stayed on their farm until he no longer had the strength to work. He had taken care of many details and worked as long as he possibly could. Mom and Dad agreed that it was finally time to move to town. Truth be known, she would have been ready to move to town many years earlier, but she loved Dad, and Dad loved his farm. It was a tough move to make because it meant the acceptance of death.

Wayne is the executor of the estate, and he went out to the farm to discuss details with them. Normally when anyone stopped at Mom and Dad's, it was necessary to find Dad before you could talk to them. By the end of May, he was normally in the bedroom resting. Changes aren't easy to accept. Witnessing Dad lose his ability to be fully involved in life was tough for all of us. He was amazing because even as his livelihood diminished, Dad continued to begin each day with, "This is the day the Lord hath made, let us be glad and rejoice!"

Vince, the youngest of our family, had expressed interest in taking over the family farm when Mom and Dad were ready to move into town. Wayne told them all to get together to talk. Vince and his wife, Amy, lived in town and were willing to switch houses with Mom and Dad. The legalities of the swap began and the ultimate home improvement project was underway. In less than a month, my family came together and refurbished an entire house. Living an hour and a half away and being the least into home improvement projects, I have to admit I was amazed!

The Tuesday after Memorial Day, the family gathered at the "town house" to gut all the rooms, with the exception of the master bedroom and bath. Those two rooms served as the living area for Vince and Amy for the next 28 days. The recently redone master suite was deemed okay by the clan. The sacrifice Vince and Amy made was regarded as a noble gesture of love not soon forgotten by any of us.

Manpower was abundant and "doing something" for Mom and Dad was something everyone wanted to take part in. It eased the helpless feeling. We gathered with numbers from 30–80, depending on what day it was and who could get off work for longer than the weekend. Dad picked up trash and threw it into the dumpster, tried to help with boards, and contributed in any way that he could. He wanted so badly to be a part of things, as he always had been before. He moved slowly and with pain. We only knew this because of the grimace on his face: never did he utter a complaint. He led prayers throughout this time and remained the wonderful patriarch of our family. His presence was enough to suffice.

We didn't want or need him to work. We just wanted him to stay.

Fortunately, my siblings are talented and have varied skills. John is in the cabinet making business and has been a carpenter for many years. Wayne owns and operates a plumbing business in our hometown. Joe is an electrician and a finish carpenter. Bob is a farmer and can do anything he needs to do to get the job done. Vince works manufacturing trailers, but also has the skills needed to work on any project. Diane, Marlene and I all work in the elementary school system and know how to use elbow grease. And our husbands chipped in as well. Our sisters-in-law dug in and proved their love for our family over and over again. Steve and Carol both live out of state and had a difficult time being a part of this project. Truth be known, they probably had an even more difficult time being away from it.

Put that line up to work, along with 30 plus nieces and nephews, and watch things happen! Mom had tons of decisions to make. The wall color, the light fixtures, the carpet, the tile, the mantel–it was like building a brand new house. Truly, it was a labor of love. My very "doing" family knew how to take care of this kind of business. It focused us all on something positive.

Twenty-eight days after digging in to gut the town house, it was a finished product. This was a beautiful house for Mom and Dad to move into and enjoy. We were together as a family more that summer than we had been since growing up together. Mom loved the new house, but the reason it was all happening was difficult to ignore. Dad continued to lose weight and spend more and more time in bed.

A family came together to work for a common cause: a project to honor our Mom and Dad. Many positive moments were shared. However, the sadness from knowing why it all was happening was almost too much to bear. We found reasons to laugh. A woman new to town asked about the "habitat" house. She had no idea the Mitchell family was so big. The nosy old-timers drove by dozens of times a day. Through the stress underlying the project, John seemingly had a need to take charge and earned his nickname, "Little Napoleon." He is the oldest and is a great project coordinator. Many jokes were told and many tears were stifled. Love was shared.

The house was ready for my parents to move in. Forty-two years of life on the farm needed to be packed up and moved into town. It was another project to tackle; another move toward accepting death.

Chapter 11

"God bless everyone."

Father's Day had always been a big deal in our family. Anything that celebrated family was important to us all. Father's day of 2003 was difficult to celebrate, yet impossible to ignore. Although the house project was in full swing, we stopped long enough to celebrate the man whom we all loved and didn't want to let go. Everyone knew that this would be the last Father's Day we would be spending with Dad on earth.

We also were dealing with the transfer of the home place from our folk's to Vince and Amy's. It would still be in the family, but it wouldn't be Mom and Dad's house any longer. Losing our childhood home was nothing compared to losing Dad.

The norm would have been to eat a large lunch together and share the whole day. Dad wasn't feeling up to an entire day of anything, so we cut the celebrating short. He couldn't eat much but still enjoyed ice cream. So it was homemade ice cream in the late afternoon. The celebration would be shorter than usual, but full of sentiment and love for Dad.

Almost everyone in the family made it. It was a nice day and we all sat outside, visited and ate. We'd all realized early on that photographic moments with Grandpa were limited, so we marked every occasion with many snapshots of Papa Ray. Grandma and Grandpa posed with all the grandkids from the various families. Next, it was time for a pic of the kids. At 40, I'm still a "kid" when it comes time to take pictures with the Mitchell family.

Chloe was the youngest grandchild at the time. She was a beautiful baby. Grandpa had a special place in his heart for all of his grandchildren, but had dubbed Chloe his "littlest angel." He was frail and weak and couldn't hold her on his own any longer, but would have Mom place her in his lap. They would sit together very contentedly. She seemed to settle his soul a bit.

Dad tired easily and quickly. So we tried to be happy, but knew not to linger too long. He needed to rest. So many things were different now. Dad had always taken naps: five minute naps after lunch on a hard floor. By Father's Day, his naps were much more frequent and much longer in duration. No amount of sleep could take care of the tiredness, the weakness, the pain or the fact. Cancer was taking him away from life. The days were heartbreaking because the sparkle wasn't evident in his Irish eyes. Frustration increased on the part of all. We wanted to take the illness away. We wanted to take the pain away. We wanted to take it all way. We just didn't want cancer to take Dad away. Although sorrow shared is supposed to lessen the load, frustration shared doesn't feel like half frustration. Many of us were thinking that with all the technology and advances in our world today, there are too many folks still dealing with the loss of loved ones from this thing called cancer.

The celebration broke up so Dad could rest again. The mood was low enough we didn't return to the house.

The zest to move them was there. The needed energy wasn't. Until living through this experience, I never knew how much vitality a terminal illness took from everyone affected.

We celebrated Dad on that Father's Day. We mourned him too. The father we'd known for so long was no longer with us. We were still very thankful for the skinny frail man who was still praising God and living each moment to the fullest, but our strong, ornery, lively little man was definitely changing before us.

Chapter 12

"Let's pray."

Moving day came bright and early on June 27th. We descended upon the farm in large number with trucks and trailers to pack up Mom and Dad's belongings of years. We had lots of help—the grandkids showed up in force, and they were put to work. We loaded all the treasures with care and took them to their new "town home." Dad had gone to lie down. Despite past efforts to be a part of the action, he was unable to pull it off this time. In a flurry of commotion, most everything was out of the farmhouse by noon. Janet and Diane pulled cleaning detail at the farmhouse so we could get Vince and Amy in that afternoon. We all ate lunch in Mom and Dad's new garage, trying to get used to the new surroundings. Dad came out to join us and made sure that we said a prayer before we ate. After lunch, some stayed to unpack under Mom's direction. The rest of the crew went to the farm to unload Vince and Amy's belongings. Dad was enjoying seeing his family working together for a common goal, and rested in his new bedroom for a while after lunch.

After most of the work for the move was completed,

we made their new home "official" with a limestone rock in the front yard. All the kids had gone together to get the family nameplate for Mom and Dad. Wayne used his backhoe to take out Vince and Amy's rock and to hoist the new one in. Mom and Dad were more than proud to stand beside the "Mitchell" rock in front of their new home for a picture. We then went out to the back patio for a little relaxation and nourishment. And then came some more surprises . . .

Chapter 13

"I almost blew the surprise three times today 'cause I opened my trap!"

Marlene and Elma had a mission from Dad to go and get Mom a new piece of furniture for the house. When they were shopping, they decided that with Mom's nice deck on the back, she needed some patio furniture. So when we were all sitting on the deck, Wayne pulled up with the new patio table and chairs. Mom couldn't believe it! She was thrilled and said that we had gone overboard.

But little did she know, she was in for one more big surprise. While some of the kids were outside enjoying the new patio furniture, some of the others were bringing in a new loveseat and chair for Mom–courtesy of Dad! We put it in place, and then Mom and Dad and everyone came in. Mom was elated!!! When she found out it was from Dad, Mom–who doesn't normally show lots of emotion–was obviously touched. It was a memorable day for sure. Everyone worked hard, and went home that night with a sense of satisfaction and accomplishment.

The sweetest part of the whole thing was the way

Dad thought of Mom and how to surprise her. He told Wayne he wanted to get her something for the house, so Wayne said we could take care of that. Dad got a pillow from the couch and snuck it to the basement so Mom wouldn't know. The night before the move, Wayne stopped to get it and threw it in his truck. Several of the brothers and sisters were sitting around at the new house, watching the carpet layer and talking about how to do things the next day. Elma thought she would go get the pillow and we could decide on colors for the new furniture. She came back in the house with the bag and when she took it out, she thought Wayne had picked up the wrong bag. She pulled out one of Dad's nice shirts, buttoned up around the pillow! Dad wanted to be sure that Mom wouldn't see the pillow if she happened to see the bag, so he camouflaged it!! It was priceless. We all looked at the shirt in amazement. We laughed and cried at the same time. Visions of Dad, his frail little frame even making it down to the basement, were a little too much to think about. He was so ill most of the time that he had trouble getting out of bed, but he spent all of the energy he had to make the move for Kay just a little more enjoyable.

The day of the move, Mom was confused because seemingly Marlene and Elma had skipped out. Dad asked Wayne many, many times from bed how the shoppers were doing. He couldn't wait to surprise his Kay. Marlene told me about letting Dad know they had made it back and Mom was going to be happy. I remember hustling back into the bedroom to tell Dad that we made it back. I will never forget the glisten in his eyes as I told him about our adventure, and how pleased Mom was going be that he was so generous. Dad was talking in a rather excited voice and I realized that Mom was just in the next room. I put my finger over my mouth so Dad would know that we probably should quit talking about the big surprise.

His reply was so Dad. "Dang! That's about the 4th time today my mouth has come close to getting me in trouble!"

The pillow, with the shirt still on it, had a special place on the new loveseat for several weeks to come. Everyone that came to visit had to hear the story. The next day there was a Broxterman reunion in the Frankfort City Park. Dad and Mom went for a while, but didn't stay too long because Dad wasn't feeling well. They went back to the house, but he didn't get to rest all that much. Throughout the afternoon, several from Mom and Dad's family stopped to see them. Rosie, Lucille, and Bette (Dad's sisters) also came to see Mom and Dad and the new house. It was good to see him enjoying all the great stories they shared. We all laughed and enjoyed the time together. Dad's sister Bette had come from New Mexico, and even though it was hard to see Dad like that, she was so glad she came. They took pictures and made more memories. Mom was very proud of her home, and Dad was happy to have her settled in town.

Chapter 14

"We need a manager in here. And a bouncer.
Let's get Chris in here to be the bouncer."

Dad was having more and more hard days, but lots of people stopped to visit. Dad had always loved to gab, so this helped the days pass a little more quickly. Charlie and Rita came to see him almost every day. They were a constant source of love and support. You could see how much they loved Dad.

Diane loved the fact that Mom and Dad were only a block and a half away now that they lived in town. She stopped by almost every day to say hi and to help Mom if needed. Mom was still going through stuff from the move. She gave it to the missions or to "Let's Help" in Topeka. Dad thought it was very important to give to those who needed it. Keith and Diane would stop often when they walked in the evening. Wayne and Elma, Bob and Cassie, and Vince and Amy would drop by often to see Dad and Mom. The rest of the brothers and sisters came on the weekends, or whenever they could, to visit with Dad and Mom and see how things were going.

Mom's brothers and sisters were great about coming to see them. Dad's sister, Rosie, was a frequent guest. She and Dad would discuss things only they could remember, like their parents, siblings, and childhood days. Family was always important to Dad, and he was important to them, too. Many of Dad's nieces and nephews took advantage of the last months he would be with us. They came to tell him he was one of their favorites. He loved it when they came.

The Scott family was a special treat for Dad. Sally Scott, Mom's sister, and her kids would ride about 60 miles on their Harleys to visit. Dad would muster the energy to walk outside and check their bikes out. He thought it was an honor to have them make a big deal out of coming to see him.

On the Fourth of July, Sally, then 77, rode on the back of a Harley for 60 miles with all of her children to visit Mom and Dad. I was there that day. We heard the roar of the motorcycles and went to the window to check them out. It was a nice treat to see them pull into the drive and know the day would pass a little more quickly for Dad. There was a bit of teasing back and forth. Sally, "Harley Granny," was chastised about needing to wear her helmet even if it might muss her hair. We all sat in the living room with Dad, sharing their favorite memories of him.

Father Bill was one of Dad's favorite people on earth. He would stop and check on Dad often, and Dad just beamed every time. Father told us it made him stronger in his faith every time he was around Dad. Dad talked to Father about how he hoped he would make it to Purgatory (of course we all knew Dad had a special place in heaven already!!). Father Bill laughed and told Dad, "If you have trouble getting to heaven, then I don't have a chance!" Dad was surprised and pleased to know Father Bill felt he was a good person. His humility sometimes prevented him from knowing how truly special he was.

Many visitors experienced difficulty to witness Dad in these last months. When Mom and Dad had moved to town, one of Dad's friends stopped by to talk for awhile. Dad had gotten really thin and was bedridden by this time. Dad's buddy and he talked for quite a while. Dad got tired and said he needed to rest. As Dad's buddy was leaving, Mom was out on the porch. She thanked him for coming to visit, and when he looked at her, he had tears in his eyes. He said, "I just can't take this." It was the last time he visited with Dad. It's one of those things that was tough indeed. Even though Dad was a tiny man, his presence in life was large. Witnessing the state of existence life placed him in at the end was difficult even for those of us who were with him every day.

My father was a long standing member of the Knights of Columbus. A fellow member visited Dad one day. He presented Dad with an award for recruiting the most new members during the last year. Dad had talked to a couple of his grandsons and a few of their friends, and had encouraged them to join the local chapter. Dad was proud of the new members for taking that step. He was proud of the award. It was evidence of his evangelizing.

Genitha Horigan was an elderly friend of both Mom and Dad. They had known her for a long time and thought the world of her. She was a very witty person and they had lots of laughs together. They went to ball games and to church functions together. They shared meals and most importantly, they shared their faith. When Dad and Mom moved to town, Genitha was a frequent visitor. She came one day with a cake for Dad because his birthday was coming up. The three of them visited for a while, and when it was time for her to leave, she gave Dad a kiss on the cheek. She then gave Mom a hug, and asked her, "Does it bother you when I give Raymond a kiss?"

Mom answered, "No, it doesn't really bother me."

Genitha then said, "Well good. I was going to suggest that if it did, you could just go out on the porch til I'm finished." Mom really got a kick out of that. Genitha passed away just a couple months after Dad did, and at her rosary service, her son told the story about giving Dad a kiss. It is comforting to both families in the community to think of Dad and Genitha visiting now with Jesus.

Whenever someone came to visit, Dad would always ask them to say a prayer with them. Father Bill shares the story of Dad soon after he was bedridden. Father was going to visit and was worried that Dad might be down. He said a few prayers to have the right things to say, and be prepared for Dad not to be his usual gentle, happy self. Father walked into the house and back to the bedroom where Dad would spend the next 4 weeks. As he walked into the bedroom and spotted Dad, he was amazed with what he saw. Dad was lying there with a huge grin on his face and he proclaimed, "Father, I'm evangelizing!"

"How are you managing to do that, Raymond?" asked Father. He was thinking of the limitations on being in one room, in bed, and surely feeling down some of the time.

"No one gets out of this room without praying with me. I ask and they have to say yes. I'm dying!"

Chapter 15

"Is there anything we need to say to one another before this all happens?"

After the move to town, the decline of Dad's health was fairly quick. Harvest came and went, and Dad only made it to that final harvest one day. Wayne drove him out to see how things were going but he didn't seem too interested. It was not his to worry about. His harvest this August wasn't of crops, but of souls. He was worried about bigger things than yield and markets. Dad needed to take care of what he knew was the most important thing in life—relationships.

Whenever there was a spare moment that summer, I took off to go visit Mom and Dad. Most frequently they would have company. With as large of a family as we have, being alone with your parents is never a common thing. My siblings and their spouses, the grandkids, aunts and uncles, cousins, friends–so many people wanted to visit Dad.

The day came when I pulled into the new house and noticed it looked pretty calm. As I walked in, I found my sister Diane helping Dad. Mom had either gone to church or the grocery store. Those were about the only times she ever left

Dad's side. When I got there, Diane headed home and left Dad and me alone. She'd already had the conversation with Dad and sensed the need for that time for Dad and me.

It got to the point we all seemed comfortable on Dad's bed. Although we had never been the type to share the family bed, it just seemed fitting to crawl onto the bed and lie next to Dad. I was lying next to Dad and we were just visiting about nothing and everything. They were desperate conversations people have when we know time is limited.

Dad cut to the chase quickly and asked, "Anna, is there anything we need to say to one another before this happens?"

It was one of those times when my inside voice didn't come close to matching my out loud voice. Inside I was screaming, "NO!" From my mouth I heard, "Dad, we've always been friends, even when I was a teenager. I know I haven't done everything right, but you've always been my friend."

Dad scoffed, "You haven't done everything right? I haven't done everything right!"

I went on to say I didn't like what was happening, but I knew we'd been lucky as a family to not have had to face death or tragedy for so long. I told him I was going to miss him and didn't know what to expect when the time came. I began to cry. It was a fairly soft cry, trying to hold in the body wrenching sobs that were just beneath the surface. I knew Dad didn't need to witness that and feel the helplessness of not being able to fix what was hurting one of his kids.

Dad, in his very delicate state, moved with what must have been excruciating pain to roll towards me. He wiped a tear off of my face and held me. More screams from my inside voice raged inside. "Oh my gosh, this man is tough! Give me strength to take this with love, appreciation, and maturity. I don't want to lose him. What will I do without him?" Thoughts raced through my mind and I didn't know what to say or do. We just lay there together, me crying, Dad comforting me for a few minutes.

Mom came home, and the day progressed as what we then knew as the norm. We visited, shared something to eat, took care of Dad and then in the evening, started receiving guests who had come to see Mom and Dad.

I decided to drive home that evening as the house filled with family and friends. I needed to drive. Alone. I needed to cry, sob, scream, and let out all of the feelings that I couldn't deal with in a full house. I did all of that and called my friend Kelli to tell her about the day.

I had to share my awe. Who was strong enough to actually initiate that type of conversation? How was he able to provide emotional strength for me? I knew that similar conversations had to be taking place. Dad loved all of us. It was tough to make it through one of those. How could he be having those talks with all of us?

Conversations between my siblings and me since Dad's death have confirmed the hunch that he had similar talks with each of us. None of the conversations were exactly the same because he knew each of us. He knew our strengths and he knew our weaknesses. I think he must have known what we could handle and what we needed. It was as if he took us to the edge of it, knowing that in the long run, it would be one of those conversations held close to our hearts for the rest of our lives.

It may be the single most painful conversation I've ever had. Tears fall each time I think about it. It is the most powerful conversation I've ever had. It was a gesture to show how much he thought of others, how much he loved his family, how much he wanted us to know peace. If only I could aspire to live like that each day, giving to others without thinking of myself. Dad was able to think of me during his pain. He showed me how much he loved me, despite the fact he must have been worried about his own death. The act of rolling towards me and wiping the tears from my cheek will forever be etched into my soul. In spite of his pain, he was compassionate and wanted to take mine.

For John, the situation seemed similar. He and Dad were lying on the bed just visiting. John is the eldest and he was telling Dad all the wonderful things he remembered from his childhood. He talked and talked about tractors and trucks, things they did together and all the ways John looked up to Dad. John finished his walk down memory lane with a question, "We were pals, huh Dad?"

Dad allowed a tear to fall at that. Although he didn't cry much, there were times that moved him. John's ability to recollect all the wonderful things he experienced with Dad as a young boy touched Dad's heart. In this case, John gave to Dad. I'm quite sure John received in that exchange as well.

One of the moments that meant a lot to Bob was very different than those experiences. Since they were partners, it takes place within the business of farming. Bob had shouldered much of both farms and was trying to keep up as best he could. It's tough to run one farm; I can't fathom trying to take care of two.

Dad followed the Broxterman way in a few ways. One of these was the way he put up hay. Dad took a couple extra steps in the process and felt it was the ONLY way to put up hay correctly.

It was late in May and the hay was cut and waiting. Bob was busy with a million other things to be done, and Dad decided to go to the field and rake the hay himself. In late May, Dad was already very ill. He was thin and weak, but a farmer to the end.

It was painful for him to carry out the task. He had to drive the tractor three times to the house to take naps. But he persisted. Dad turned the hay to let it completely dry before they would bale it the next day. The experience for Bob illustrates many of Dad's traits.

He was determined, hard working, and did things in the way he believed. Dad was almost selfless in his actions. Not many folks would work through pain in that way. Was it perseverance, or stubbornness? It doesn't really matter which way any of us answer that. It was Dad. He was a farmer, tried and true. For as long as he was able to move, he spent time on the farm working. It was a huge part of his identity. Bob is walking closely in his footsteps with Jack, his son, following closely at his heels.

Diane initiated her moment to express her anger about the situation. Dad ordered Carol, "Front and center! You aren't going to get out of this." As I said, he knew us each well enough to know how it had to be.

Some of my siblings are still to raw to share. I respect their grief and their way. We all proceed differently. The focus I see is that Dad loved each of us in his way for our way. He said it all. I am amazed as I look back. Those were some tough roads we traveled.

More expressions of appreciation

My mom's sister, Anna, was able to stay with Mom and Dad for much of the summer while Dad was ill. She has experience as a nurse and has been a part of the Sister's of St. Charity for forty-six years. Sister Anna (as we call her) was a great comfort for all of us during our trials that summer. She has a gift of creating the right atmosphere to allow people to be comfortable sharing their feelings. One of the first examples of her facilitating the sharing of feelings was on an evening shortly after Mom and Dad moved to town. I was not able to be there on this day, but have heard the story many times from various perspectives.

Stacey is my oldest sister's daughter. She was fortunate to have been visiting this particular evening when this sharing took place. She shared this story with me.

Diane & Keith, John & Cindi, Bob & Cassie, Jack, Chloe, Mallory and Stacey were at the new house. Grandma and Sister Anna were there as well. Grandpa had just gotten out of bed for a bit to sit with us in the living room. Sister thought it would be good for us all to talk about what we were feeling. She told us that people are often taken from our lives unexpectedly, and we don't get a chance to prepare ourselves for the loss we will face. She explained how lucky we were to have that chance to say goodbye and let Grandpa know how much he meant to us.

We went around the room and each person got a chance to tell Papa Ray (as well as everyone else) what we were feeling about his sickness and the thought of his not being with us. We got to tell him what he meant to us!!

Stacey's dad Keith started. He had barely begun to speak when he started crying. Tears were running from everyone's eyes. He told the story of when he dated Diane and how intimidated of Papa Ray he once was. But that no matter how intimidating Ray was, Keith had an unbelievable amount of respect for him. Keith spoke so many kind words about wanting to live more like him in a Christian way. Grandpa was the reason he chose to convert to Catholicism and to have Papa Ray as his sponsor.

They moved around the room, hearing stories of the kids growing up. There were chuckles of fond memories, but all of those chuckles were through tears. It was really hard to look at Grandpa and tell him all of your feelings that had been bottled up, because it meant you were saying goodbye to an amazing man. There was no doubt he knew how you truly felt.

It was an amazing night, and everyone present felt so

incredibly lucky to have been a part of it. There was but one wish they all had: that it could've been an evening when more people were there to share that much more. It would've lasted all night long. Stacey was the oldest grandchild there, along with Mallory, Jack and Chloe. Even though they were very young and too little to join in the conversation, it was incredible to see how attentive they were. All three of the little ones were well aware of the sadness and the emotions that ran through the room. Each of them actually went to Stacey on the floor and sat on her lap. They sat quietly, listening and watching. It was extremely awesome to Stacey how they came together to sit with her. They realized that each of their parents was consoling one another, and they were drawn to Stacey for some reason. There was a definite bond formed between everyone in that room. It was an amazing evening.

It was hard on both Grandma and Grandpa, but it also helped. Crying is definitely a good thing when there is something like this that we are forced to deal with. Papa Ray sat, attentive to what everyone had to say. Each time someone complimented him on being such an amazing, hardworking, loving, caring soul, he would simply nod his head and say "Thank you" and "I love you."

Chapter 16

"Good people. Wonderful people."

Dad had lost more weight, was now in bed all the time, and was not up to having any sort of celebration for his upcoming birthday. Father's Day had worn him out, even though we were there for a limited amount of time.

We decided to hold a card shower for Dad to celebrate his birthday. We called the Mitchells and Broxtermans, and we placed notices in the local newspaper and in the Summerfield paper (where Dad had graduated from high school). We were hoping for a good show to let Dad know how much he meant to so many.

The cards started arriving a couple days before Dad's actual birthday of August 7th. A few were funny, most were nice, and many were full of emotion and love. Dad received over 200 birthday cards before it was all over.

My sisters and I were appointed to read the cards to Dad. We would show him the card, read the message, and then read the personal message. We would read for 15 to 20 minutes and then allow Dad to rest. Each card brought about a positive comment from Dad. He needed to share what good people the senders were. He had something nice to say about everyone who had written to him. Dad had a kindness in his spirit that brought about kindness in others.

Reading those birthday cards was no easy task for my sisters or me. Many of them were full of expressions of love, and some told of how much Dad would be missed in the upcoming months. You could hear the emotion in each of our voices as we read personal messages like these:

From Amanda, a granddaughter:

Grandpa,

> *This card just couldn't have put it any better. You are simply an amazing person. My admiration for you really can't be measured. The dedication you have to the family and to God is truly inspiring. I love you Grandpa, Happy Birthday, Love Always, Amanda. . . . Dad gave some positive remark about how hard Amanda worked in school, or what a beautiful spirit she had, and commented about what a good girl Amanda had turned out to be.*

> *The others in the room would cry. Diane, Marlene and I would signal when we'd had enough; then it was someone else's turn to read. These were among the toughest days to endure. As people were sharing their feelings for him, we were realizing even more what a wonderful man we were honored with as our father.*

> *With emotion putting big lumps in our throats, we'd read on.*

From John, the eldest child:

Dad,

> It's times like this that make us realize more about the
> way we should live every day. You've been an inspi-
> ration to me my whole life. I didn't know you could
> possibly be more until now. You are my hero! I love
> you more than you know! Happy Birthday, John

> *The cards kept coming . . .*

From Mom's sister, Sister Anna:

Dear Raymond,

> Since your "dating days" with Kay, you have been
> one of those sturdy and bright sunflowers for me.
> Your most significant likeness to a sunflower is that
> you have followed, in your own spirit, the movement
> of the Son. Thanks for being an inspiration to me all
> my life, and thanks now for living your dying days
> in such a way that each of our journeys has been
> enhanced.

> *Love you, Anna Marie*

Dad inspired so many people. An opportunity to share your
feelings for someone important before they die is a gift,
albeit a tough one to deliver. Some people from many years
earlier took the time to send Dad birthday wishes.

From a friend from forty years ago:

Hi Jeff (Dad's high school nickname),

I fixed your machinery for many years, and now I wish I could fix you up one more time and right now. And I wouldn't even charge you anything!

Your blacksmith,
Tinker

Many were tough to continue reading . . .

From Charlie and Rita (brother and sister-in-law):

Ray,

Ever since we heard of your illness we have been thinking of how far we have traveled together, the sights we have seen, the times we have laughed together, cried together, and solved all the world problems—if only we could have gotten someone to listen!

We will miss having you with us, but I'm sure you will be here in spirit. You have been an inspiration to us all. Hopefully we will travel our journey as well as you are doing. We love you and will pray for you and Kay. Love and Happy Birthday, Charlie and Rita

I remember reading that one. Charlie and Rita were

in the room. It was so difficult to read about missing Dad after he died when he was right there with us. It was surreal. How could this really be happening?

There were some from his nieces and nephews addressed to their favorite uncle; one from the dogs they had to leave on the farm; and some from friends of ours because they knew what we were going through, and they knew how much Dad meant to us.

From Dave Meusborn (a soon to be grandson-in-law):

Ray,

I will never be able to fully tell you how I feel. I love your family and often find myself amazed at the way they come together. Their strength is a product of love. I see the grace of God in your eyes and feel love in your voice. I want to tell you that I'm forever touched by having known you and will always remember you. God bless you.

Love,
Dave Meusborn

And from a grandson who truly does emulate Dad in many ways, even though he is a very young man. He holds the same wisdom, the same insight, and the same gentle kindness.

From Dusty (a grandson):

Grandpa-

> *Growing up, you have always been someone I have looked up to and admired. You are so hardworking, always have a funny story to tell, and you have always had great advice to give out. I have a tremendous amount of respect for you, and I would consider it to be a great accomplishment if I turn out to be half the man you are. I love you, and happy birthday. Dusty*

> *Dad's sister, Betty, sent one that was much needed as comic relief in the midst of some very raw intensity. She is Dad's oldest living sister and lives in New Mexico.*

From Betty:

Raymond,

> *Have a good day today and remember what Sister Josephine used to say. If you get to heaven before I do, throw down the rope and pull me through!*

Love, Betty

Reading over 200 cards, feeling that much emotion, and listening to Dad making a comment about every one of the people who sent cards made for lots of time spent with Dad. Instead of wearing Dad out, the love being sent, along with his family being near, seemed to rejuvenate him.

On the evening of Dad's birthday, his bedroom was the most happening place in town. You have to remember it is a small town, but we still packed 30 to 35 people in one bedroom. Dad loved having his family close to him.

This particular night, Dad must have felt entitled to ask for what he truly wanted, and he wanted us to sing. And so began one of the first nights of song. Andy, one of my nephews, decided to go to the church and borrow several hymnals, so we would at least know some words to the songs we were singing.

Dad was lying in bed, arms stretched up and out, and he began directing his choir. He had always loved music but had never been as forward about requesting it. He not only requested certain songs, but went as far as asking different individuals to sing.

Dad requested that my uncle Linus sing. He has a great voice, plays guitar, and is Dad's "cowboy buddy." I keep expecting him to head to the bluegrass festival to be one of the entertainers, but so far he only does small requests for those he loves. Following a few songs by Linus, we all sang again. Then he asked that Craig and I sing "How Great Thou Art" for him. In the end, we sang and prayed and laughed for hours. It got late enough, we worried that Dad should be sleeping. But it was hard to leave, and Dad seemed to truly enjoy the evening.

Every once in awhile someone would joke about Dad's choir of crows, but to Dad it was heavenly music. The stress of the move was out of the way, harvest was not his worry, and his family was all gathered around him. Dad's sparkle in his eyes, the grin on his face, and the readiness to celebrate life and change the world returned. He seemed to know that he had some influence, and truly could make the world a better place for us by emphasizing how to treat one another.

Dad had a great birthday that year. It didn't matter that he was restricted to his bedroom. He was in his glory.

He directed his choir, he shared his love, he was able to pray with everyone, and he was told over and over again how much he was loved. He had his entire family gathered around him and eager to listen and meet his requests. He never once spoke of pain, fear of death, or self pity because he couldn't get up any longer. He did speak of God's love for us and God's wishes for us to love our fellow brothers and sisters. He modeled prayer as a powerful tool to relieve anxiety and stress. He shared his humor. He was grateful for the life he had. Each and every day, Dad continued to be thankful for the gift of life. "This is the day the Lord hath made, let us be glad and rejoice."

Chapter 17

"Isn't this a good day to die?"

Although it seemed incredibly unfair, life continued pluggin' away, even though Dad was lying in a bed dying. School was revving up for another year. Although it was heartbreaking, my sisters and I had to get back to our schools and get things ready for the upcoming school year.

It was a very strange time in life. I never felt like I was in the right place. While I was in my own home, I felt the need to be at Mom and Dad's. While at their house, I felt as if I should be at home, getting ready for school. It left me with an unsettled feeling 100% of the time.

Dad was strong in spirit and mentally very aware and alert. No one knew how long he could carry on. I didn't want to miss out on a thing, but life doesn't let you call in sick when you have a classroom needing your attention.

I forced myself back to Abilene and began preparations for the school year. I made the best of the short time I'd allowed myself to take care of all of the before-school activities–copies to make, lessons to plan, curriculum to map out, and a classroom to prepare.

Our school district meetings began on Aug. 14th. We always start with the entire staff of Abilene School District getting together to introduce new staff members, hear the superintendent speak about the upcoming year, and take care of any other details pertaining to the entire staff.

In Frankfort that morning, things seemed to be changing. My niece Amy was lucky enough to be there with Grandma and Grandpa. She recalls, "Grandma and I sat next to the bed as Grandpa was waking up. Lying there so peaceful with his hands clasped resting on his chest, he opened his eyes minimally and asked, 'Is this purgatory?'"

This caught our attention. We looked at him intently to determine if he was enquiring of the present, or dreaming out loud? Is he now confused and disoriented? He looked at Grandma and said, "Well, this can't be purgatory. It's not your time yet Kay. And Amy, you are too young to be here. So I guess this isn't purgatory yet." Then he closed his eyes again.

Grandma and Amy sat there in silence. Then grandpa began speaking to deceased relative aloud. "Hey there, Alfred! Hi Ves! Where's the ice cream? Hi Sister Vera, hello Bud, and there is Jon (Charlie and Rita's son)." He spoke to them briefly and mentioned a few other names. We sat in awe with tears rolling down our faces. Grandpa was back and forth between his bedroom and heaven that morning. He spoke of heaven, and that he felt that day was the day he would join the Lord in heaven. It was amazing how many emotions one can experience at the same time. Amy shared that she was scared and sad, yet at peace. She was happy for Grandpa, yet selfishly she was not ready to give up Papa Ray!! The hospice nurse had informed Grandma that many times patients know when their time has come, and it was apparent that Grandpa felt differently today than any day before. We did not want anyone to miss the opportunity for their last moments with Grandpa, so we decided to go with it. Grandma and Amy discussed it briefly and decided to call in the troops. It was a day of anticipation in that every minute seemed so important. No one wanted to leave his side in fear of missing out on something he might say. We checked on him so often that day that his naps were not of any quality. All the brothers and sisters were notified and were making arrangements to get to Frankfort ASAP. Grandpa was in and out of heaven, but thankfully God blessed us with his presence for several more days."

During this time, I was at my school district meetings in the physical state, but mentally I was very much with my family and thinking about Dad. The meetings dragged on, and that misplaced feeling was very much with me. As the morning wrapped up, I was called to the office and found my husband in the foyer. He was holding his cell phone and looking at me with deep concern. "Honey, your Mom called. Hospice thinks your Dad will die within twenty-four hours. He's seeing heaven. Your Mom wants you all to come home." Craig told me as gently as he could, but you can never be prepared for something like this, even when you know it's inevitable.

I immediately started crying for fear of never seeing Dad alive again. We crawled into the car and took off from the meetings. Craig pushed the speed limit all the way to Frankfort. He instinctively knew it would have crushed me not to be able to see him alive one more time. I needed to say goodbye.

We were used to the scene upon arriving at Mom and Dad's house: many cars, lots of family, and no one really wanting to say much. We took the direct route and headed to Dad's bedroom. Expecting to see Dad unconscious and near death, we witnessed a surreal scene. Dad was propped up with nurses on either side of him. He was very pale and weighed less than a hundred pounds by that time, yet he looked entirely peaceful and serene.

As I walked into the room, I fell with relief into the chair nearest the door. I was thankful to find Dad alive and shocked to find him so full of a strange sort of vitality.

Dad said, "Okay, almost everyone is here now. Anna, isn't it a good day to die?"

How does anyone answer that question? Inside my head I was screaming, **"No Dad!** Just hang on! We want you **here**! We **need** you here! I can't even imagine you NOT being here!" Instead, I simply shook my head yes and let a tear roll down my face.

Dad responded to the overt sadness. "It's okay. Your classroom is empty this week. You don't have a room full of kids yet. This is a perfect day to die."

It was incredible. In his pain and time of trial, Dad was worried about **my life.** He wanted to get this dying thing done, so we could all go back to our respective lives.

Little did I know that Dad's time on earth wasn't nearly over. He had so much to share, so many folks with whom he had to share God's word with, and so many more lessons to teach his loved ones.

After several hours of praying with Dad, visiting with family and feeling emotionally drained, I decided to walk to my sister Diane's house for a short break. As I was walking, my sister, Carol, and her husband, Rich, met me in their car. They were finishing their 7 and 1/2 hour trek after getting the same phone call about Dad.

The look of anxiety on Carol's face matched the fear I had experienced earlier that day. I eased her fears. "He's still here. He's waiting on all of us to arrive before he goes."

Without a word, Rich drove on. Carol had that very same need. She had to see Dad alive again. She wanted to tell him goodbye and thank him for all he was.

When all the kids' grandkids, aunts and uncles, friends of the family, Father Bill, Sister Anna, and Mom gathered round my Dad's bed, it was a bedroom full! We'd all grown up with the large family scenario and knew how to pack in pretty tight. My estimate at the high end of visitors in ONE bedroom is at least 50 people. Mom usually sat on the bed next to Dad, one of the kids next to her, with our spouse behind us and our kids by our sides. Repeat that 9 times and throw in Charlie and Rita, Father, Sister, and various other visitors at any time, and you can imagine the group.

No one wanted to miss a moment. Dad started to share wisdom and express thoughts and feelings like he'd never shared before. It was at this time I knew I had to write a book. I knew at gut level there were things being shared that needed to be recorded.

With the family gathered by his side, Dad became more forward with his wishes and threw caution to the wind. He wasn't exactly taking what he needed from us, for he was giving us all gifts as he asked us to pray or to share or to sing. He led us through his dying. He shared with us so much faith.

Kneeling around Dad's bed, with all of my siblings and Mom holding hands, sent me back to being five or six years old in an instant. I could see us all 30 years younger on our knees, praying the rosary and reading the Bible. We did this nightly. I'd always thought it was Mom that was the leader of the faith. Dad's death showed me that it was a shared responsibility between him and Mom.

During Dad's final days, we all held hands, bowed our heads, and connected in a spiritual way. The common prayers that Catholics are sometimes faulted for became a mantra of sanity. Those prayers allowed us to share in a way that was comforting to Dad, Mom, and each of us. Those community prayers connected us as much as holding hands and sharing memories of long ago. It was the first time I truly understood the power behind praying in that manner. Our subconscious prayers became clearer as our community prayer soothed our souls. Through prayer, singing, and sharing our love for our folks and our family, we were given the gift of actually seeing a living faith. Perhaps there was a doubting Thomas among us. Maybe Dad knew that someone he could reach actually needed to see faith, but I know that it strengthened the faith of each of us in the room.

As the family gathered, Dad rallied a bit. His vitals improved, and even though he was ready to die, it wasn't going to be that day. He wanted to die, he wanted to allow us all to get on with life, but he wasn't finished teaching us. He wasn't finished with his family on earth.

"God, are you there?" Dad was feeling a little anxious about not being in heaven yet. He was seemingly on earth and in heaven at the same time. He had a foot in both worlds. He was lucid and aware of his surroundings in both places. Dad greeted each of us as we'd walk into the bedroom, and he noticed when we left. Yet he was talking almost constantly to God and others that had passed to the other world, from a few years to decades ago.

His first and frequently repeated question was, **"God, are you there?"**

When he first began asking this, we all tried to answer him. "Yes, Dad. God is here." I can't even attempt to guess how many times he asked us that in the first couple days of trying to die "right." The question changed slightly to things like, **"Three divine persons in one, are you there?"**

As we continued to answer, Sister Anna and Father Bill decided that Dad didn't want us to answer. He was waiting for God's answer. The roles of Father and Sister became Dad's personal spiritual advisors. We needed them. We weren't dealing with a typical death. Dad was trying so desperately to "do this right" that we needed their guidance as much as Dad did.

We left Dad's questions unanswered. The only reply to "Are you there, God?" was the frequent, blaring, and lonely whistle of the train bearing through town just a block away. For a bit, Dad began to relate that sound as God's answer.

He posed his question yet again. "God, are you there?" Silence. Dad hesitated only a moment, and in a sing-song voice said, "Heavenly train, don't fail me now!"

Dad apparently got an answer from God at some point. He asked, **"Are you there, God?"** No one answered, but Dad went on. **"Good, I'll try not to make any more wise cracks!"**

His one-liners always brought about relief for everyone in the room. He had us all right where he wanted us. Dad also decided the trains were the town of Frankfort's purgatory. After spending forty-five years in the country, the noises in town were a bit distracting.

We all discovered how much Dad loved singing and music. He had always liked Johnny Cash, and while he was in the train mode he sang "Hear that Train A'Coming." His monotone voice seemingly disappeared, and he sounded amazingly musical! Carol told him she thought he had a promising career in heaven. Dad said, **"I don't wanna take any of his fame, but I think I sing better than Johnny does."** Dad had been humble his entire life. This statement was BIG; his confidence was high.

The family would take breaks to eat, use the rest room, catch our breath a bit, and give Dad some time to rest. Each night, we reconvened to pray, sing, visit, and listen to Dad's tale of his journey towards death.

All along the journey, Dad was concerned about each one of us. He wanted to ensure that we were all going be okay without him. He said things like, **"Is everybody** happy?" "Do you have freedom?" "Make it count!"

Dad wanted to make a difference on a grand scale before he died.

"**I'm ready to change the world. Anybody with me?**"

We were all rather overwhelmed with the emotion and apprehension about losing Dad. Evidently, it affected our response. Dad had never had a formal coaching role, but you'd have thought it was his lifelong career that evening. When our response wasn't zealous enough, he'd ask again, louder, "**IS ANYBODY WITH ME?**"

We learned to answer, respectfully and with fervor, "Yes, Dad! We are with you!!!" No room for doubt.

On this particular night (Aug. 14th), however, Dad wanted more than his family. He needed to talk about things of major importance, and he wanted someone who was going to help him make a difference. We needed a priest or a nun! He held them in reverence in all ways. The family rule was to always treat them with respect, reverence and honor. He knew we were with him, but we needed someone to lead us. Although Sister Anna was with us most of the time those last couple of months, there were a few times Dad was left wanting, and this was one such moment.

In his struggle to work through things, Dad said, "**Amy, call the Pope!**" Amy struggled along, but gave up and asked for Grandma's assistance in this matter. No matter how hard she tried, she couldn't talk Grandpa down. Mom tried to explain to Dad that we couldn't get through to the Pope on the phone. Dad said, "Get a penny, we'll flip for it." While Mom wanted to help him, she declined, not knowing how to handle it if Dad won the flip. Dad called her a chicken.

Dad finally gave up on the Pope, but wanted someone of importance to discuss change in the world. Unfortunately, Father Bill was on vacation in Colorado for a short break, and no Sister Anna.

"I need somebody big!" Mom decided to call the priest who was covering for Father Bill while he was in Colorado. Much to our gratitude, Father arrived at the house. We were all shocked at Dad's reaction to this priest. Dad was always kind TO EVERYONE. However, the questions at that time were only, **"Can you give me Father Bill's number?" "Where is Father Bill?" "Is there anyway you can get Father Bill for me? I really need to speak to him."** The priest did his best to comfort and console Dad at this time, but Dad couldn't be satisfied. He needed to speak to Father Bill before he could go to heaven. Father was not only his priest but also one of his closest friends. The priest filling in for Father Bill left and apologized to Mom for not being more helpful.

Dad was absolutely determined!

Chloe, Dad's littlest angel, entered the room in someone's arms. She was about seven months old at the time. Dad spotted her, pointed to her, and announced to everyone, **"She can do it. Chloe will let Father Bill know I need him."**

Although Dad was certain this would happen, the rest of us were uneasy and worried that Dad would be upset when Father Bill didn't show. We ended that evening with more prayer, more singing, and lots of hugs and tears.

I doubt any of us slept very well that night. Colorado seemed like a world away, and the likelihood of Father returning before Dad died was very dim.

Chapter 18

"Chloe will call him on the heavenly cell phone."

Early the next morning we had a visitor. Father Bill came through the door of the house with urgency to see Dad! He told us he felt the need to be there for Raymond. He had driven through the night to get to Dad. The word from hospice was that Dad would die anytime. It was a miracle for Dad to have Father Bill there for him. We were amazed and so relieved. Dad was not surprised in the least. He thought perhaps Chloe used a heavenly cell phone to get in touch with Father while in Colorado. He knew his "littlest angel" Chloe Marie had gotten the job done.

"I think we ought to listen more to the little people. I want you all to understand Chloe's language. She hasn't been out of heaven very long," Dad tried to explain to us.

"She is closest to me in age. She just got out of heaven and I'm on my way," he went on. This was a new thought from a man we'd known for all of our lives. It was intriguing to hear, and it felt like he had this information from a source bigger than we could comprehend.

However it had happened, what we witnessed was unbelievable. Dad told Chloe to get a hold of Father. Father drove through the night to get to Dad before he died, and he had everything with him that he needed to say Mass. Mass was held in the bedroom for Dad's benefit. In the Catholic faith, August 15th is a holy day. It is called The Feast of the Assumption of the Blessed Virgin Mary. This celebrates Mary's happy departure from this life.

As we celebrated the Mass, Dad listened carefully even though he couldn't participate much. During the message, Father suggested that perhaps Dad should be referred to as "Saint Ray," patron saint of hospitality. Dad raised his hand to protest and tried to speak. Father laughed and assured Dad he wouldn't canonize him but would, indeed, call him Saint Ray when he remembered him. Dad calmed down with a smile on his face.

To some, it seemed a perfect day for Dad to die. I remember his sister, Rosie, saying it would be just like Ray to die on a day of celebration for Mary. Dad had always been very much into the rosary. The rosary is a process in which Catholics pray. We said it at least daily while growing up. Mom and Dad had the timing down to an art. If you began to pray as you left the garage, the entire rosary could be recited before you made it to church. On long car trips, we would stop everything and pray the rosary if it happened to cross either of our parents' minds. We said it as a family at night on our knees, in the living room before we went to bed. It didn't matter what TV show was on, or if you had homework!

The rosary was now a way to calm Dad down and enable him to actually get some rest. My brother, Wayne, caught on to this and would often start the rosary for us to pray to quiet his thoughts and give him peace. This makes me smile! I remember being teased when I was young about this kind of thing. If my older brothers and sisters would try to get ready for bed too early, I'd tell Mom and Dad so we could pray before they were asleep. I'm sure Wayne was a contributor to the teasing, and here we were; he was starting the rosary!

Dad had visitors throughout the day. We allowed him to rest, but the day was once again filled with many interesting stories. As evening came, the family crowded around and we had another night of singing, praying and visiting. But still Papa Ray held on.

Chapter 19

"This is my miracle"

It had been months since anyone had mentioned the miracle we'd all prayed for and wanted so desperately. However, with Dad confined to his bed, too many people in a house that was newly built, and the saddest time of our lives upon us, Dad claimed that he had indeed received a miracle. Not THE miracle, but a miracle nonetheless. So many prayers had been offered for Dad, and he believed they were not wasted. While many of us were scared about losing Dad and upset that he was surely going to die, Dad was looking at God's graciousness and love.

He claimed the miracle of our family as his miracle. And it was, of course. For he and Mom are to be credited to the whole thing. But as Dad saw us all packed in his home together, laughing, praying, loving and believing, he claimed it as his miracle.

The small town we grew up in is still home for many of my family members. This allowed us all to stay in various houses in guestrooms, on floors, in campers, etc., to be close to Dad and Mom during this time. During the day, we'd reconvene at Mom and Dad's new house and hang out. It was a very strained, odd, wearing time.

While it was great to be with the family, we couldn't escape the fact that we were waiting for Dad to die. No amount of love, prayer, laughter or faith could have alleviated that pain. However, I cannot fathom that time if we hadn't had huge amounts of all of those.

Dad witnessed all the children he raised with all of their spouses, children, and grandchildren, gathered round him. He had us right where he wanted us. If he wanted to sing hymns, we sang hymns. If he wanted us to pray, we prayed. If he wanted a drink, there were plenty of us to offer him the sponge "lollipop" with water. The whole family hung on his every word, and we would have done anything within our power to fulfill his desires.

Dad's biggest concerns at this point were that his family would be okay without him, that we would join him in heaven someday, and he would die right. He worried some about dying well. He was never afraid of the afterworld, but wanted to go out with dignity, with each member of his family drawing near to God.

I have learned since Dad's death that he wanted to reconcile each of us with the Catholic church. His spiritual advisers, Father Bill and Sister Anna, led him back to knowing that faith was in God, not in religion. Dad also wanted to single-handedly fix the problems and scandals in the Catholic church. He was very worked up about it and had to be led back to letting go and allowing God to work those things out.

Dad wanted to know many things before he left this life. One of the less personal yet intriguing questions he asked was about the seeming disappearance of all the money in 1929. He was bothered by "how was it all just gone." He asked my sisters and me, and although I tried to research this for him, I couldn't really satisfy his question. It was something he must have always wanted to understand. He remembered losing the house Grandpa and Grandma had built during the 1920s and having to leave that farm. I think it was a shattered dream for his whole family, and he lived with that his whole life. I know he had done many things for his father, but I'm sure he felt helpless that he couldn't do more at that time. His early experiences would have an impact on the way he lived the rest of his life. Dad was admittedly a miser, and he was pleased that Mom was so good at being frugal as well. He obviously worried about her when he was gone.

Mom bought a candle that was similar to a vigil candle and told Dad. It was during the time the family had started praying for Dad to go to heaven. His pain was increasing, and he had lost so much weight that there was nothing left. He didn't eat and he could only suck on a sponge for water. His body was deteriorating, and it was just time. Mom prayed around the clock and told Dad while he was awake, "I've had a candle burning for you for the last two days."

While we expected a "thanks" or an "I appreciate that," the answer was, "You need to watch out for your economy."

Besides the economy, Dad's random questioning continued.

"Is this heaven?"

"Did I tell you I made it to heaven?"

"God, does this have to be so scary?"

"Do you have freedom?"

Occasionally we would interact with these questions. At one point Dad was saying, **"Consider us. WE are in heaven. It should get to lookin' more like it."**

Bob, always ready with quick wit and a smart mouth, said, "Yea, I thought it might be bigger." Being packed in the bedroom was always an interesting venture, and some comic relief was always appreciated.

Dad loved to laugh, and appreciated the place of humor in all situations. He heard someone laughing and asked, **"Who is the good laugher here?"**

My sister, Marlene, told him it was me and said, "Anna."

"Bless you, Anna. It is so important to laugh. Laugh in front of your boss when he needs a laugh," Dad directed me. I've always had a loud laugh. Some folks say it's musical and seem to enjoy it with me. I've fought the thoughts that it's too loud and obnoxious. Now, as I'm laughing from the soul, I think of Dad and never worry.

My brother-in-law Keith spent many nights visiting with Dad along with the rest of us. He loved Dad like his own father. He'd been in the family for a long time and was familiar with the dynamics. He was sitting close to Dad and saw Diane, his wife, walking toward the bedroom. He said, "Here comes a beauty."

Dad saw Diane walk in and responded, **"You ain't just beatin' your gums together!"**

Another time during some friendly family banter, someone called Keith "buggy." Dad was quick to defend his son-in-law with, **"Keith may be a lot of things, but buggy isn't one of them!"**

We shared our feelings with Dad during these hardest times as well. We shared verbally, with cards, and by trying to do things that made Dad happy or comfortable. He was good about accepting most things, until we got carried away with telling him how wonderful he was. Then he would inform us we weren't to tell people that. **"You need to tell people I'm a rat fink. That way, they'll pray for me."**

While Dad accepted prayers in his behalf, his attention was often on Mom. Mom was with him in many ways.

She was his nurse, his partner in all things, his friend, and his love. There wasn't anything they weren't involved in together. Amy verbalized it well when she said we'd all been privileged to watch them fall in love all over again. Although they'd had their share of ups and downs, I felt like they'd had a strong marriage. Their faith and strength allowed them to look at the positives while Dad was still alive, and that enabled them to grow together even more near the end.

Dad received the last sacraments a few times when hospice thought time was almost over for him. Mom was always right there beside him. She loved him and supported him through it all. **"It's okay to go to heaven now, Ray. We'll miss you, but we'll be okay."**

"I'm here. I'll be here til the end, just like you asked me to be."

Dad missed Mom's presence when she wasn't in the room. My sister Carol and my brother Steve were staying with Dad through the night. It was one of those nights he talked nonstop, and they tried to calm him down and get him to sleep. He really didn't want to sleep and was rather put out that they wanted him to. **"Man, that sleep must be a pretty important thing."**

He asked them where Mom was and they told him she was sleeping. It was less than two minutes later that he repeated, **"Where's Kay?"**

"Dad, she is sleeping," Carol said, trying to get him to understand.

"She sure does sleep a lot," was his response. It was obvious he was most comfortable with her at his side.

Dad gave us so much by being in each moment and sharing his thoughts and prayers with us, but gave us even more when he shared his visits to heaven.

Chapter 20

"Did I tell you I made it to heaven?"

For nearly two weeks, it seemed that Dad was both in heaven and on earth as he wove in and out of consciousness. Although many nonbelievers will chuck this up to morphine or that he was not lucid, that is far from the truth. While he was using meds to control his pain, he was mentally aware until his final three days.

Dad tried to describe his foothold in both places to my sister-in-law, Janet. **"I'm here, I'm there. It's confusing."**

During this time, Dad talked constantly. At first we tried to answer him to satisfy him. When we realized we weren't what he needed to satisfy him, we allowed him to converse with God.

He would wake up and ask, **"Are we in heaven? No, this is the old bedroom. Thanks Vince and Amy."**

Usually he was content, but occasionally there was some frustration on his part because he was ready to go home. **"I need to get on with this transition." "Don't wanna mess this up." "I wanna do this right!"**

Although he never complained, Dad was obviously aware of his physical appearance. He was talking aloud in a semiconscious state and asked, **"Am I still skinny? Do I have a decent body again?"**

Dad confided in Father Bill regarding things of heavenly nature. Dad was a thinker and questioned lots of thoughts and ideas throughout life. One of his questions was whether he needed to earn God's love, or if it was a constant. Dad went through a time of spiritual warfare as he wavered in his thinking. Sometimes Dad felt God loved him for being him. Other times he felt the need to try to be perfect to earn God's love. We knew that Dad found his serenity when he reported to us that he was where he wanted to be.

"Did I tell you I made it to heaven? Heaven is so big. God answers me so fast, I have trouble understanding. You wouldn't believe. The devil lost. Have an invitation to the heavenly banquet. I want you all to join me at the heavenly banquet. There's no room for prejudice of any kind at God's banquet. Do you hear me? No prejudices. I've found the path to heaven. It's in a pasture north of Vliets! I want the path to be wide enough for everyone to go with me."

After he felt comfortable with his journey to heaven, Dad gave us advice that seemed bigger than any other advice he'd ever given any of us before. **"Make it count!"** Dad had always encouraged me to use the gifts God had given me to enrich the world. I felt like he was emphasizing this point. I felt like he finally realized that he had made a difference in many people's lives, and he wanted us to each minister in our own ways as well.

"Take care of those closest to you." Dad wanted to go home to Jesus, but was having a difficult time leaving his family. He was trying to get things all in order. Having us take care of one another allowed him to move on through his transition. I feel his push every day for many reasons. It's on my heart to help Mom get through this change. It's also on my heart to forgive myself, and everyone in life thus far. Dad's ability to forgive was remarkable. Before I took off for New York to volunteer at Ground Zero, Dad encouraged me to forgive Bin Laden. His influence will be with me until my own journey is over.

"Maybe we ought to listen to the little ones." It was obvious he had a newfound understanding of very young children, being closer to God. He thought they had a special language. To enter heaven, we must become like little children. Dad achieved that in his attitude, his humility and his gentle, playful spirit. It was apparent in his smile and his youthful appearance. His body had shriveled to the size of small boy and was no longer of use to him, yet his face literally was childlike. He was weak and in pain, couldn't eat or drink, hadn't been out of bed in weeks, and somehow appeared full of peace and serenity. He knew he was going to see his best friend, Jesus. He had never been more certain that God would not let him down.

"May the Lord be with you. I was always kinda shy about saying that . . . I didn't feel worthy." Dad had a unique humility about him, but he finally felt like he was an example for the Lord.

"God Bless everyone." He wanted all of us to get a glimpse of what was in store for those of us he loved and had to leave behind. He also shared a few things to look forward to as we sought the kingdom of heaven.

Sister Anna was the first to go in to check on Dad one morning. Upon entering the room, she was informed that Dad had talked to Jerry the night before. Sister was a bit shocked and in disbelief. It was rare that anyone mentioned Jerry. He was the man she had been engaged to nearly fifty years earlier. He was killed in a farming accident. Dad had visited with him in heaven.

It was difficult for some of us to believe Dad was truly IN heaven, because we've all been through enough to be doubtful. Dad was testing our faith in yet another way. He was faithful, he believed, he had no doubts, and had made it to heaven. We were witnesses to his pre-visits to his life in the hereafter, and it was up to each of us to believe.

Dad spoke to many family members and friends that had passed away before him. We heard him talking to his folks. **"Hi Mom and Dad. Am I doing okay down here? Am I doing it right?"**

One of Mom's brothers died in 1990. Dad greeted him by name. **"Well, there he is. Hi Bud, you ol' devil."** Uncle Bud was ornery like the rest of Mom's brothers. I thought it was a funny way to greet someone in heaven, but very fitting to how Dad was in life.

Dad's sister, Rosie, has always been very close to our family. She was present during much of Dad's last weeks. As Dad was visiting others in heaven, she inquired about her late husband, Mac. "Raymond, do you see Mac up there anywhere? I'm not at all sure he made it," she said in her usual joking manner.

"Yeah, he's here," Dad said as he smiled and reassured her in his quiet manner.

One morning as Mom and Diane were back helping Dad, he told them they were beautiful. Dad was doing his best to love Mom enough so she could carry his memory in her heart. He complimented her and cared for her as best he could. **"I have some beautiful angels helping me here this morning, but earlier I saw one even more beautiful."**

Mom inquired to whom he might be speaking about, and Dad replied, **"Mary."** Mary had been a devotion of Dad's for many, many years. He had learned this from his mom, and she probably from her mother in turn. Although misunderstood, if you look at any belief or devotion from the perspective of what someone was taught and raised in, it is understandable. Dad had seen the mother of Jesus in heaven, and it was a very happy day for him.

Though Dad was concerned with two worlds at that time, it amazed me that he was still very much a farmer at heart. It was a terribly dry summer, and the need for rain was apparent to all. Dad would mention how dry it was often as he was preparing for his journey to heaven. The closer he got to God, the more confidence he gained. He began to tell us that he would talk to God about some rain. We would all laugh and encourage him to do just that.

He also asked that before anyone drank alcohol the evening after his funeral, that we each have a personal conversation with Jesus. He made it clear he wasn't talking about a prayer that had been memorized, but a heart to heart. He wanted us to have a talk with our friend. He was still working for the Lord.

Perhaps the most amazing visit Dad shared was with my Aunt Sally. My Mom's sister, Sally, had suffered a heart attack the first week in August. Although all indications were that she would recover and be fine, Dad was worried. Each time we gathered to sing, pray, and visit, he would be the one to remind us all to pray for Sally. Dad may have had some sense of things not known to the rest of us. We had been reassured she was going to be fine. She suffered another heart attack less than two weeks later. This was about the time Dad was awake and aware for the very last time. He was so very weak, and we were praying for God to take him home. No one, young or old, was holding on to false hope. We knew he was ready and needed to go.

The morning we received word that Sally had passed away, we discussed the issue in hushed voices, far away from the closed door to Dad's bedroom. It was decided there would be no reason to share the sad news with Dad. He would be extra worried about Mom. Losing her sister and husband within the same week was a difficult load to carry, and Dad didn't need the extra worry.

Father Bill came to visit that morning. As he entered the bedroom, Dad volunteered, **"I saw Sally in heaven. She was with Jesus. They are waiting for me."**

It was at this point that doubt vanished for me. I had wondered before but now, how could I doubt him? Dad was actually visiting heaven. He was still teaching us. I'm sure he knew there were a few of us still doubting. Dad was working for the Lord. As Father Bill said later, "If Raymond could have won one more soul for the Lord, he would have gladly suffered longer."

Chapter 21

"Jack, we don't want to slight anyone, anytime.
I don't want anyone here to be slighted ever in your
whole life."

Papa had a bond with each of his grandkids. They endured this summer of Dad's illness and death. Young and old, they were with their Papa Ray through it all. It gave me a lot of hope in the next generation. Not only were they present, they wouldn't have missed it for anything. Although this was the toughest time of our lives, they showed character by being there all the time. They worked next to us, prayed next to us, cried with us, and consoled us when they knew we needed it.

Mallory, Jack and Chloe were all very young, but very much a part of things and important to Dad. One of the amazing characteristics about Dad is that he valued everyone: young and old, family or friend, all races and religions.

Dad was sensitive enough to know his appearance was not what it had been. The decline of illness has a way of scaring kids who are too young to comprehend. Mallory became a bit shy, and acted nervous about getting too close to Papa Ray since she didn't see him every day.

"Let's throw bashful out. You don't have to worry about anything, even if I'm not the most handsome man in the world."

Dad wanted the kids around and wanted them to be comfortable. Chloe was constantly on his bed with him. She sat contentedly. She was a great source of joy and pride for Dad.

Jack, Chloe's big brother, is a farmer through and through. He had a special place in Papa's heart as well. He loves John Deere tractors just like Grandpa and loves Papa—with all of his heart. Jack wanted to share something, and Dad was more than happy to clear the stage for his favorite little guy.

"Let's let this little guy say his night prayers for us all. He can't be bashful. We threw that out."

Jack, who was three at the time, had changed his nighttime prayer without prompting. He changed it to, "Mathew, Mark, Luke and John, bless the bed Papa lays on. Four corners to his bed, four angels overhead; one at the head, one at the feet, and two to guard him as he sleeps." He recited that prayer in front of the entire family for Papa. It was a frozen moment in which fifty people stilled and let silent tears flow, without worry about who might see.

Dad wanted to make the path to heaven wide enough to allow all of us to get there. He repeated this often. He so desired to take his family with him, but knew it was his job to plant the seed for each of us to eventually make it to be reunited with him someday. **"I want the path to be wide enough for everyone to go with me. Heaven is so big, you wouldn't believe."**

Dad had faith in his grandchildren. He wanted them to take care of things for him and do their part to help out. You could hear him making requests of them, and they'd do their best to grant his wishes.

For Chris, when the room was packed full: **"We need a manager in here. Call Chris, he'll be the bouncer."**

For Stacey, Papa Ray had a special challenge. She had just graduated from college, and he wanted to know she was going be successful. **"Stacey, did you get a job? By the way, I have a couple of things I think you could do. Invent a clothing line that will cover up women's bodies, a breath mint that will work for up to ten miles, and a prop to hold up sick people so the nurses won't have to."**

For Amy, who was a nurse and worked full time during Papa's time of need, a special bond developed. She was by his side when she wasn't at work or sleeping. They shared lots of talks, and he obviously valued her word. One day when she was back in the bedroom with him, she asked him if he was going to heaven. She said he opened his eyes and said, **"Yes."** He went back to sleep but woke up seconds later and asked, **"That's okay, isn't it?"** Dad really wanted the family to be able to handle it when he left.

As a special treat to their Papa Ray, Amy and Stacey sang to him one night. There is a popular country song by the Judd's called "Grandpa." The words are printed below. There was not a dry eye in the house that evening. Dad didn't cry often, but during that song, a tear fell silently down his cheek. Another moment frozen in time.

GRANDPA

Grandpa, tell me 'bout the good old days
Sometimes it feels like this world's gone crazy
And Grandpa, take me back to yesterday
When the line between right and wrong
Didn't seem so hazy.

Did lovers really fall in love to stay
And stand beside each other, come what may?
Was a promise really something people kept
Not just something they would say?
Did families really bow their heads to pray
Did daddies really never go away?
Oh, Grandpa, tell me 'bout the good old days.
Grandpa, everything is changing fast
We call it progress, but I just don't know
And Grandpa, let's wander back into the past
And paint me the picture of long ago.
Did lovers really fall in love to stay
And stand beside each other, come what may?
Was a promise really something people kept
Not just something they would say?
Did families really bow their heads to pray
Did daddies really never go away?
Oh, Grandpa, tell me 'bout the good old days
Oh, Grandpa, tell me 'bout the good old day.

Chapter 22

Go Mitchell Maniacs!

It's hard to fathom how much emotional pain Mom endured during this difficult time. Her husband of fifty-three years was bedridden and dying of cancer, and her sister had just died of a heart attack. She couldn't leave Dad's side to attend her funeral. It was incredibly heavy, and even though she had nearly sixty to ninety members of her family around her every day, no one could help her carry that sorrow.

We divided for the day. My older siblings left to attend our Aunt Sally's funeral, while the younger five of us stayed with Mom and Dad. It was a tough decision for each of us.

Dad was now with us only in the physical state. He no longer spoke and rarely awakened. It was very difficult to go back to the bedroom. I felt he was gone. Sister Anna thought perhaps Dad needed this extra time because he was visiting with each and every person he saw on the way to heaven. It was his way in life: why would this be any different?

Sister Anna had gone to be with Sally's kids during their time of sorrow, and returned to be with us after Sally's funeral and burial. She became somewhat of an angel to all of us in both families. She had lost a sister, and was losing a brother-in-law who was in her life since before she was out of high school. Yet she served as our rock. I cannot remember her crying. She was celebrating that Sally was with Jesus and that Dad was on his way. It was amazing.

A *Relay for Life for Cancer* event was being held in Frankfort the same day of Sally's funeral. We had decided to have our team months before. After everyone was back from the funeral, questions started coming up now and then about how to handle the 'Mitchell Maniacs' participation in the event now that Dad was on the edge of death.

The track where the event was to be held was only a block away from Mom and Dad's, which made it easier to participate. So we decided we'd all go down and walk as much as we wanted as we alternated shifts of being with Dad. We wanted to participate, but not be away from Dad too long.

The relay was a beautiful event. The night was perfect for it. If our hearts hadn't have been broken, we would have enjoyed it all very much. From the front porch of the house we could see and hear everything. There was music playing and hundreds of people walking and talking. It was confusing to see happy people as my Dad was in the bedroom dying. Life must go on.

As we would walk down to walk a lap or two, the people in the community would stop and ask how Dad was and extend their sympathy. It was tough. It was so good of them to care, but what can you say at that point? We are praying for him to die. We want his suffering to be over. There will never be words to express what our loving, gentle Irish leprechaun meant to us. But the community cared for Dad a great deal as well, and they needed to know.

The lights went off and the only images anyone

could see were of the beautiful luminaries. The names of the people who had died of cancer and those who had survived were announced. Other than the announcer's voice, the entire place was silent. The names went on for well over an hour. In my head, I couldn't imagine the pain of so many people from one disease. And, this was just one county in Kansas. I tried to imagine the number of people affected in all of Kansas, or the country. It's impossible to know or comprehend the number of us in the world affected by this terrible thing called cancer. It's too much for anyone to try to think about or feel. My thoughts returned to Dad.

Mom came down to walk a lap while the lights were off. It was good for her to get out for just a few minutes. She became my heroine through this ordeal of Dad's illness and death. She has strength of unknown limitations.

The announcer came to Dad's name and the luminaries were lit in his honor. The announcer's voice broke, and she had to stop for a moment to gather her emotions before she could go on. She's a close friend of some of my older brothers and sisters. I'll never forget that moment. It was exquisitely painful and comforting at the same time. As she said Dad's name, and you could hear the emotion in her voice, it felt like the world stopped for just a moment, and all of the energy in the universe was feeling for Raymond Mitchell.

She went on to tell us that everyone was thinking of us and praying for Dad. Hang in there, Ray. It's almost over. Another moment frozen in time for us. It was one of those times being from a small town was a huge blessing.

After the intensity of those moments passed, we all dried our tears. It was good to have the lights come back up. The music started and the walking began again.

Most of us were exhausted, emotionally mostly, so we had made the decision to only walk a little while and then go be with Mom and Dad. We left a few at a time and went on with life as we knew it then. We drifted off to the various houses and turned in for the night.

My sister, Marlene, hung in there a bit longer than I. She has always walked during stressful times, so this was a good outlet for her. She noticed at around 11:00 p.m. that her kids, Dusty and Amanda, along with Daniel and Amy's boyfriend Dave, were taking turns running laps instead of walking. The plan was they would run five and then walk five. Dusty and Amanda had been cross-country runners, and they were using this outlet to deal with their grief.

Marlene finished 100 laps and decided to call it a night. She walked to Diane's to crash on a couch for the night.

She remembers being awakened at about 4:00 a.m. by a very excited Daniel. There were people sleeping on the floor, and Daniel was trying to roust his brother Luke into getting back up to run. He told him they needed a few more of our family members to go walk because the "Mitchell Maniacs" were in a tight race to win the award for the most laps walked.

It was confusing because most of us had called it a night early. For the most part, it was four team members who had relayed for us. Marlene decided to get back up and rejoin the team.

As she walked back to the track she could see a lot of activity going on. A couple of her friends approached her and told her through tears that her kids were "machines." She looked at the track to see Dusty, Amanda, Daniel, and Dave still running. It was now 4 a.m. and they were still running 5 laps, walking 5 laps. They had never stopped.

Dusty saw her and said, "Mom, I just can't stop running for Grandpa! I just can't stop running."

Amanda–always full of spunk–ran up to her, gave

her a quick hug and said, "Gotta' go. Mom, I love you." Marlene told me she thought of the Energizer Bunny as she was running off.

Members of other teams were donating laps to the Mitchells because they had figured out these four runners were trying to win this relay for their Grandpa Ray. There were people tossing water bottles and cheering for them as they ran by.

Marlene was crying again. It was a mixture of sadness for the losses we were enduring, but there was also tremendous pride for her kids and her nephews, and their labor of love for Dad.

At 6:00 a.m., at the end of the event, the laps were counted. The "Mitchell Maniacs" had come in first place! They had done it for Grandpa! As the awards were given, Dave asked the rest of the foursome if it would be okay to give the pizza party they'd won to the second place team, who happened to be a bunch of younger kids. They'd worked hard too and it wasn't a prize the Mitchell team had been after. The kids that took second place cheered and were elated to be rewarded with a pizza party for twenty! The joy awarded to those four who had each logged 38 miles that night will last forever.

As the story spread through each of the houses where we were staying, pride in who those kids were was a wonderful emotion to mix in with the sadness that seemed to have been burying us. Grandma Kay was **soooo proud**! We all cried, there were lots of hugs exchanged, and the story was told over and over. It was such an exciting morning. It was a much needed bit of relief. Go Mitchell Maniacs! Go Dad! GO DUSTY! GO AMANDA! GO DANIEL! And GO DAVE!

Chapter 23

"May the road rise to meet you,
And may the sun be always at your back,
The rains fall soft upon your fields
And until we meet again,
May God hold you
In the palm of His hand."

Dad was still hanging on to life–barely. He hadn't had any food for ten days, and the only water was from a sponge. He hadn't been awake or aware of anything as far as we knew. None of us knew how long it might continue. Our lives were in a time suspension.

Many of us headed out to go to our homes and try to get our worlds in some sense of order, knowing the time was near. But no one could predict when Dad might pass from this world to the next. There were things that each of us had to do to continue to put our lives on hold. Life forces us to move on.

I called some of my friends to help out with some emergency lesson plans. We worked as quickly as possible, and then I went home to take care of the essential chores. I called Mom. Things with Dad were exactly the same, so I decided to sleep in my own bed before making the trip home. Several of my siblings had decided to do the same, to get some rest to endure the inevitable.

Although it was difficult to sleep, I must have managed because the phone startled me awake at around 1:30 a.m. It was Craig. He had stayed at Mom and Dad's; his experience as an EMT enabled him to help Janet, Amy, Mom, and Joe care for Dad through his final days. It was as if Dad had needed most of us to be gone before he could leave. His suffering was over.

At the time, it was a relief. Dad had suffered too much. He had lived two weeks past the time Hospice had first called us all home. It seemed Dad rallied when he had his family around him. We all knew he was now with Jesus. He and Sally were visiting and joining all of our other relatives. Dad no longer had his shriveled body, and his pain was gone. We were sad that he was gone, but we never would have wished for him to spend one more moment enduring the pain.

I drove home early the next morning, letting tears fall freely for the full hour and a half. It wasn't an easy trip. I knew the next several days were not going to be any easier than the last two weeks had been.

Arriving in Frankfort felt surreal. Could it still be home without Dad? We had lots of family around. We had the normal sixty to ninety that we'd gotten used to, but now we were calling in the extended family as well. Aunts and uncles from both sides were coming in preparation to attend the services. It was hard to grasp it would be because **my** dad had died. He would have so enjoyed the entire family being together. He would have talked for days. His spirit was felt, but his smile, the twinkle in his eyes, his unique monotone voice—everything about our beloved Papa Ray was missing.

When I drove up to the house, being with family made things feel better.

Even without our sweet, loving, gentle father, our family was going to be intact. It would take some adjusting to figure out who we were now. There were questions that will remain unanswered, hurts that will never completely heal, and lives forever altered by the death of one amazing man.

Inside the house was louder than it had been in months. There were hustling and bustling bodies everywhere getting things done. There were folks receiving food and supplies from the community, writing down names, and starting thank you notes. Others were calling people who were from out of town and needed to know Dad had passed away. My sister was collecting pictures to make a collage of Dad to display at the dinner after the funeral. We'd all sat around waiting and worrying for so long, it seemed odd to see everyone busy.

The community supported us with more than ample food and supplies to accommodate all the guests for Dad's services. We received plants, memorials, cards, and sympathy from hundreds. Dad's life had touched so many.

The story of the time of his passing came from a few people who had been there when he died. It's another of those mixed feelings for me. I am not sure I would have been very strong for Mom had I been there, but at the same time I feel a bit regretful that I wasn't there. It's hard even now to think about.

My brother Joe, his wife Janet, and Amy were with Dad the night he died. We'd all been praying for Dad to go home.

Amy told Joe and Janet that we'd prayed to God, we'd prayed to Mary, we'd prayed to St. Francis, and maybe it was time to pray for some personal help up there.

Sister Adrienne was Dad's sister who had died of cancer in 1986. She was a wonderful woman. She was ever faithful and had a sense of spirit that was a breath of fresh air. It was she that Amy suggested they ask for a little help. Using the idea that Betty–Dad's other sister–had written about in her birthday card to Dad, they asked Sister to throw down a rope to pull Dad through. Amy then prayed, "**Sister, pull harder! Pull harder!!**"

Amy shared the story of how she remembers the night Grandpa died unfolding,

"It was late, around 12:30p.m., and I thought I should head over to Mom's(Diane's) to change into my p.j.s. I was quietly visiting with Joe and Janet, and had just kissed grandpa on the forehead, then proceeded to put on my shoes. As I was putting on my shoes, Janet quickly said, 'Amy,' and I looked at Grandpa. At first I noticed nothing, but then he struggled for a breath. I realized he had a period of apnea (not breathing), and then another.

"I asked Joe to get Grandma and Janet and I talked to Grandpa, telling him it was ok to go to heaven.

"Grandma rushed in and with a weak voice said, "It's ok Ray, go on in to heaven."

"We sat with him, crying and reassuring him as he took his last breaths.

"Mom was at his side telling him how much she loved him, as Dad finally let go and left this world. Family gathered all around him as Mom prayed the Irish prayer, followed by the Serenity prayer."

Outside on the porch, Vince, Andy, and Dave were still visiting. Father Bill had just left for the evening. Dave shared his memory of the same evening, "Father Bill had just left for the night. Father wasn't just a priest. He was a part of the family at that point. He meant the world to Grandpa, and that meant a great deal to us. We decided it might be a good time to pray. They proceeded to recite the 'Our Father' together. It was less than two minutes after we finished our prayer that Amy came to the door to tell us of Grandpa's passing into heaven."

When Dave shared this I was amazed, and secretly feeling a sense of awe. Vince is the youngest and a very quiet guy. He is not one I would see initiating a prayer. Andy is Wayne's son. He likes to socialize, and I really couldn't see him initiating prayer either. Dave was a soon to be grandson-in-law to Ray. For the three of them to pray on their own, Dad's effect was huge. He had caused great change in many of us.

Mom praying the Irish Prayer was another factor I found awesome. My mom's family is made up of true "Dutchmen." The German pride is always there, and she and Dad used to jokingly duel over the German/Irish factors. Mom was totally selfless in her prayer choice, totally his wife and partner. It was a touching story to hear. It made me see how truly connecting a marriage can be.

After Dad was taken away, Mom crawled in the bed and went to sleep. It seemed to comfort her to be as close as she could to Dad. Her strength amazed me through it all.

Chapter 24

"I only have one chance to get this right"

It bothers me that during our toughest moments, we are expected to deal with arrangements and make decisions when it's obvious there is no earthly way we are of sound mind. The entire process of picking out the coffin and listening to the prices of what it costs to bury a loved one infuriated me. Of course, it was the first time I'd had to deal with anything like that, and my Mom had been through it too many times. She handled it all with grace and style. She and Dad had made many decisions ahead of time and had taken out insurance to deal with the outrageous cost.

My brothers dealt with everything as always before. The Mitchell sense of humor was ever-present, and probably the only way we made it through it all.

Mom was looking at very nice wooden coffins and my brothers were in the economy end of the line. Wayne said, "I know Dad would be thinking we should be looking over here."

No suggestion was going to budge Mom. She knew what she wanted for her Raymond and that was it. It didn't take too long and we were back at the house preparing for the rosary and funeral. Sister Anna was back from Sally's services and was a big help in planning and arranging Dad's services.

It was decided that we would hold a 'Living Rosary' for Dad. There were many people there. Many people were standing in the back, and chairs had to be put up down the center aisle to hold all of the people who wanted to pay their respects to Dad.

Chapter 25

The Rosary

My Mom and all of my siblings and I squeezed in the first pew. As people arrived, they each came by our pew to personally extend their sympathy and give a hug to each of us. It was difficult to maintain my composure many different times.

One of my friends, Joan, came by with a ladies handkerchief that my girlfriends thought I might need. She squeezed it into my hands as we hugged. It was very much appreciated and wiped many tears away over the evening and next couple of days. I treasure that gesture, and it rests on my nightstand next to other precious mementos of life.

Aunt Sally's kids arrived and we were all able to extend our sympathies to one another. We are forever bonded with them now. Shared grief seems to have cemented us to one another's families. Our empathy for what the other was going through has created a level of depth between us unlike anything else I've ever experienced.

As the service began, Sister explained what was going to take place. Each of us spoke about Dad, offering the bits of humor and wisdom Dad had left us with in his final days. We chose some serious things and some funny. We laughed, we cried, and we prayed.

Each decade was led by one of Mom and Dad's grandchildren.

Uncle Linus recruited several of Mom's brothers, sisters and in-laws to sing as he played guitar. They sang, "Precious Memories" and "On the Wings of a Dove." Linus has an incredible bluegrass sound to his music and it was such a comfort to hear him play and sing.

Lots of the grandkids sang "Grandpa," and there wasn't a dry eye in the church. It provided healing and comfort. It gave us a release to express our love and our sadness for Dad.

Chapter 26

The Funeral

There was even more evidence of Dad's impact on the community by the number of people present for the funeral. The church was packed and the parish hall was at standing room only.

As the service began, it was obvious that Father Bill had lost a good friend. Emotion was apparent with his every word. He started out by saying that Dad had been baptized in the St. Benedict church, but when he saw Mom shaking her head, he quickly corrected himself. He said, "No, he was baptized in the St. Bridget Church. Forgive me, Ray. I love you, Ray."

Father went on to tell the story of visiting Dad in the hospital for the surgery to deal with the colon cancer. He told Dad at that time that he was one of the best people he knew. Dad responded by singing a few words from a little tune, "you don't know me very well." Father sang the tune to us and it was just like listening to Dad. Father had Dad down perfectly.

Father's favorite memory was of Dad saying, "**Let's**

go have a cup of coffee." It was an invitation to go share coffee and conversation. Dad was always a conversationalist.

He shared the love Dad had for his family and how much his family loved Dad. He told of spending lots of time at Mom and Dad's house and described the way the family was there for support through it all. He had seen the strength the family gained from Dad's last days and was confident Dad would have suffered even longer if it could have provided more strength to us.

Many people commented on what a wonderful job Father had done with Dad's services. Everyone could tell how much Dad had meant to Father Bill. We knew how much Father Bill had meant to Dad. Father's voice broke a couple of times during the service as he spoke of Dad's faith.

I'll never forget coming out of the funeral. I went to Mom to see how she was doing. She gave me a great big hug and kept saying, "I'm so sorry." It confused me. I felt so much sympathy for her. We were all hurting and it amazed me that she could be extending her sympathy to me. She did that over and over as she gave each of us a hug.

Mom had six sons and four daughters watching out for her, but I noticed very quickly she had continued to move with the same grace and strength with which she and Dad had handled his illness. She wowed me with her strength.

The Burial

The drive to the cemetery was short, but waiting for all the cars to park took a while. The pallbearers were six of Dad's grandsons–Mitch, my son, being one of them. It was a privilege for each of them. They were proud to do this for

Grandpa. Many tears were shed, but they took their responsibility seriously.

After the all too quick ceremony was over, the time to leave Dad's body at the cemetery was upon us. This is a task I imagine is difficult for all families. Sister came through for us once again and started singing *"Peace is Flowing like a River."* As we sang, we slowly walked to our cars and departed. Although the ordeal of Dad's death was almost over, I knew the ordeal of life without him would be never-ending.

Expressions of sympathy . . .

Words are comforting to me at times when I need to be uplifted. Many cards offered our family sympathy during our time of loss, but a few stood out because of the sentiment or sweetness. I believe they deserve to be a part of this labor of love.

From a family friend . . .

Dear Kay and family,

> *Our love and prayers are with you. I feel blessed to have known Ray and to have counted him as a friend. He was loved and respected by many! His funeral was a remarkable tribute to a remarkable man. Our lives are better for having known him. He will be missed! His memory will remain always in our hearts.*
> *Paul and Judy Studer and family*

Just a note to tell you how grateful I am for having the opportunity to meet Ray. He was such an inspiration!

His funeral was awesome! I have never been to a service that had so many people there!

May God's presence comfort you.

Anita Droll (hospice nurse whom later converted to Catholicism because of Dad's influence and faith)

My Aunt Mary's granddaughter pointed at Dad's casket and told my cousin, Laurie that it looked like Uncle Ray was in a treasure chest. One of her friends relayed the precious story to us in a sympathy card.

Kay and family,

My thoughts and prayers have been with you during this time. Mary shared her granddaughter's reference to a "treasure chest" when she saw the casket . . . how true . . . Ray was a "treasure" . . . loved by his family and friends.

I'm sure your wonderful memories with Ray will help you get through these hard days. Hang in there. Ray is at peace, knowing he left a loving family.

Love, Pat

Dear Kay and families,

The verse on the obituary was excellent. It mentioned everything from prayer to Ray's visiting with everyone, his humor, his gentle nature, and his love and respect for everyone. He will be missed. I'm glad his suffering is no more!

Rachel Hunninghake

Dear Kay and family,

*So sorry to hear of the loss of Ray. He will truly be missed by everyone in this community. He was such a kind man–probably the nicest man I know. JD always knew who would be the 1ˢᵗ one to come up to him after one of his concerts with a sincere compliment and a handshake–Ray Mitchell. The little ol' guy with a big grin and a big heart. You'll never know just how much that **really** meant to JD. The next concert truly won't be the same.*

God has a good man up there with him now.

Thinking of you,
Sheree and JD Gallion and family

And possibly my favorite one . . . it succinctly says it all.

Dear Kay,

> *There's a popular T.V. program called "Everybody Loves Raymond." That title also applied to Raymond Mitchell. He left a great legacy.*

Jane Maurice

Everybody loves Raymond. We always will, Jane.

Chapter 27

"Don't wanna' spill the beans . . ."

The approaching anniversary of Dad's death was an ominous time. Something about that first year after a loved one dies . . . you don't want to linger there, but don't want to go on and lose even more of him. Because you have no choice, you keep plugging away with that date looming. Many of the members of my family were anxious. They were all worried about Mom and feeling the sadness for ourselves as well. Dad once again, even a year after his death, came through and helped us out.

Mom went to mass that morning much like any other day. It was being said in Dad's honor, and she was happy to meet Diane, Bob, and Chloe there to join her. Tears were shed as the priest acknowledged Dad.

Like most other August mornings in Kansas, it was dry. It was the same type of drought we had experienced the previous year. Rain was badly needed. Much like the year before when the rain blessed us after Dad's funeral dinner, the rain blessed us again. As the mass ended and Mom and the others walked out, it was raining. Smiles replaced tears as thoughts of Dad having a talk with God about some rain filled their minds. Dad was close to each of us that day, but he wasn't through showing us just how close he really was. The rain was only the beginning.

We all moved through our day in our various ways; teaching, running a business, farming, working on computers, etc. But for all of us, it was markedly differently. For Vince and Amy, it was **hugely** different.

Vince, my youngest brother, and his wife Amy had been in the process of trying to adopt a child for some time. I'm sure it was a process that took longer than most of my family realized. The field had been narrowed down to a precious little girl in foster care. Ironically enough, Aug. 24th was to be the day they were given the official word on Alyssa. It was uncanny. Bob, always full of offhanded wisdom, offered his two cents worth, telling Vince he had nothing to worry about considering the date. Although we all had similar feelings to some extent, it was still a tense time with something so monumental on the line.

I survived the school day reliving all of the events of the year before in my mind. Mom had been first and foremost on my mind. Arriving home for the afternoon, I began calling Mom to see how she was fairing. Several times I tried, but there was no answer. Worrying about a parent in times like this has to be payback for all the times they worry about their children as irresponsible teenagers. I tried not to worry but to no avail. I wondered where she was, if she was okay, if maybe Diane had visited and gone on a walk with her–the general questions you try to focus on without going to the extremes.

Finally, I called and she answered, but sounded out of breath. I asked her what was up with her sounding winded.

"I just walked back from the cemetery. I had to thank Ray. Vince and Amy got their girl," Mom shared.

Worry changed to happiness and joy turned to tears. I was trying to choke all the emotion back so Mom wouldn't misunderstand and get sad too. To this day, the tears I shed were sadness. I miss Dad more than words can express. There were also tears of great appreciation for feeling his presence so near. There were feelings of happiness for Vince and Amy. They were a very deserving couple who had given in so many ways for the sake of family. Now they had an opportunity to begin one as they wished.

Tears of remembrance . . ."**I can't spill the beans, but somebody has a secret,"** was something Dad had said in those last days leaving us all wonder. He mentioned another Mitchell joining the family.

For some time after Dad died, we'd ask various family members if they were expecting, but it faded and we just assumed this was one Dad had gotten wrong. The news of Alyssa transported me right back to the bedroom and the whole family surrounding Dad with love and hanging on his every word. He had been so much wiser than any of us knew.

Alyssa becoming a member of our family on the anniversary of Dad's death was a healing of sorts. I'm sure the community heard the collective sigh of relief. Never again will it be such a looming day. It goes without saying that it will always be a day of mixed feelings. Forever we will think of Dad: his spirit, his love, his sparkle, his gentleness, and his wisdom. The faith we witnessed and the lessons we learned were invaluable. Alyssa will be more than a blessing. She'll be added to the list of miracles surrounding Dad's journey. I'm not sure when we'll ever stop counting.

We got it, Dad—we know we are blessed. We'll join you at the banquet. Thanks for making the path wide enough.

Chapter 28

The Following Year:
Ray's Birthday Card & Other Legacies

Ray's Birthday Card
"Your husband, Ray"

In a world gone crazy with too many meetings, too much hype, and so controlled by media, I (along with my 9 siblings) had an amazing privilege to have "Big Ray" as my Dad. He was small in stature, yet huge in spirit. He left behind a legacy—to be simple, loving and honest, with a purpose to serve others. I'm finding out it's a challenge to follow in his footsteps. It's a challenge set by his model, as well as the amazing story Dad left us through his own journey through life and death.

This is an example of the type of simplicity and love Ray was able to share. His presence remains beyond his death as his love will remain in the lives that he touched forever. Although Dad died in August of 2003, my Mom's birthday in 2004 was not forgotten by her husband of 53 years.

Grief is one of those concepts no one can really

understand until you find yourself right in the midst of the pain. My family is no different. We can still pull together 80 to 90 people to celebrate holidays and birthdays, but there is always a longing and an ache to have the one who God called home to be here with us again. We literally "survived" that first year after Dad died. Some of us wept in solitude, some shared openly, but **all** of us were affected deeply and went through the motions of celebrations and events.

Amy spent time with both her Grandpa and Grandma, but evidently found time to talk to Ray without Kay too close in proximity. Without that time, Dad's act of love carried out over a year past his death would never have come to pass.

The whole family was ready to celebrate Amy's wedding in September of 2004. Friday evening was the rehearsal dinner, as well as Grandma Kay's birthday. We sang "Happy Birthday," did the whole cake and candles thing; and Mom received cards, gifts, hugs, and well wishes as the night went on.

The following day, we gathered in force to witness Amy and David exchange vows and celebrate in great Catholic tradition. They paid tribute to both of their Grandpas by having pictures, candles, and a special moment to honor and remember them. They were special people, and we were all missing them on that grand occasion. Tears, smiles, love, and joy were shared that day. Amy was a beautiful bride, David a handsome groom, and their day was enjoyed by all.

Mom was there as the proud Grandma of the gorgeous bride. She laughed and talked at the reception, danced a couple songs, and then went home. Mom fully takes part in all she can. It shows on her face how much she would like Dad to still be with us, but she understands life and how it must go on. She takes in what she can to enjoy life and deals with the sadness like all widows must—life as it is now without Grandpa.

Sunday came and went with Amy and David opening gifts at a brunch at Diane and Keith's home. The weekend was almost at its end . . . almost.

During Dad's final days on earth, he had Amy busy with more than caretaking. Dad was worried because it was nearing the end of August, and Mom's birthday was coming up. He knew he wasn't going to be around to celebrate with her. He asked Amy to go buy a card. She brought it back to Dad's bedroom, and he signed the card, knowing it would be delivered after he was gone.

Dad died on August 24th. Mom's birthday is September 17th. That first year, there was no way Amy was going to share that card—still too raw. Less than a month after Dad had passed away, a card like that might be too much. Amy held on to it, knowing after the first year had passed, the card would be a gentle reminder of how much Grandpa loved Grandma.

So, the big event of the wedding was wrapped up. It had gone beautifully and was enjoyed by many. During all the activities throughout the weekend, however, it never seemed like the right time to present the card. Mom would need some alone time after receiving it. Monday morning the bride had to get up and go to work, so Amy's mom, Diane, took the card to Mom. Mom was tired and already feeling a little lonely, as going to family things alone always seemed to make the loss harder. Diane went into Mom's garage where she was working and talked for a little bit about the wedding. She then told her that she had something to give her that would be hard to see, but she would be touched. Diane told Mom about when Amy was sitting with Dad one of the last days before he got really bad. He told her he wanted to do something for Kay's birthday, but that he didn't think he would be around to share. So Amy told Grandpa that she would go out and get a card for him to sign. The card itself was heartfelt, with all the right words in the poem. But the scrawled handwriting of my father with the simple sentiment, "your husband, Ray," was the most beautiful part. Diane gave that card to Mom that morning, and when she opened it, Mom put her face in her hands and wept. After a minute or two, Mom said, "I still can't believe he's gone. I still can't believe I'm a widow." Diane hugged Mom and they both cried a little more. Then they went inside the house for some coffee, and to share memories of the man they loved and missed immeasurably. Diane stayed for a long time to be sure Mom was OK. When she got up to leave, she asked Mom if she would be alright. Mom said, "I will be. Tell Amy that I love the card." A few days later, Mom wrote Amy a card and told her she would cherish the card forever.

A simple gesture shared becomes an irreplaceable treasure. Dad's love continues to shine on us.

Other Legacies

It is what we value, not what we have, that makes us rich.
~Leo Buscaglia

Linus's cross

Dad's cowboy buddy, Linus, is my uncle. He is a deep thinking individual. Linus and Ray were always the best of friends. Their conversations covered topics from the injustices in the world, to the life hereafter, to farming, and many others. They both were born with the gift of gab. More often than not, the two of them would be the last to leave a family gathering.

Along with the rest of us, Linus felt a devastating loss when Dad passed away. He was having one of his sad days, which he refers to as "bad hair Days," earlier this fall. He was out in a pasture, praying. He prayed and prayed and felt no relief, so he decided to have a conversation with Ray.

He admitted his doubts and fears to Raymond and was having a dialogue about the feelings of "is it all worth it?" and "is there anything else to this thing called life?" He asked Dad to give him some kind of sign to let him know that it would all be worth it in the end.

Linus knew he was asking for a lot. Feeling Dad was in heaven and could pull some strings with Jesus, he allowed himself the question, "Raymond, if there is something more than this, send me a sign."

No cell phones were on, no one knew where to get in touch with Linus and he spent the rest of the day with nature. Much like Ray, he was a lifelong farmer and felt most in touch with the spirit working with nature. He worked through the day looking for a sign.

Upon arriving home, Linus noticed no one was home in the usual bustling house he shared with his wife, Mary. Their children all live close and it's a bit unusual for no one to be around. He didn't think much about it and proceeded into the house. He noticed the answering machine was blinking. Not giving it a thought, he pressed the button to retrieve the message.

Amy, Raymond's granddaughter, was calling to ask Linus a favor. She wanted him to play the guitar at her upcoming wedding to accompany Craig in a solo. Linus reports that he started whooping and hollering and gave a big, **"YYYEEESSS!!!!!"** to Ray, followed by, **"I got it!!! That's my sign!!!"**

The wedding was to take place Saturday and it was a request from Craig to have Linus play. There were only four days before the wedding, and although it was nerve racking, Linus would not pass up this opportunity.

Friday night was the rehearsal, and it brought about

lots of nervousness for Linus. He felt Craig and Sarah (another musician) were way out of his league. Feeling out of place and more than a little low on confidence, Linus began to wonder about his "sign."

His wife, Mary, had to do some talking to convince him to let go of the concerns and go with the plan to play at the wedding. She encouraged and supported him, reminding him it was Craig that had requested he accompany him.

During the rehearsal, Amy and David handed out gifts for each person who played a part in their wedding. Linus received his gift and was taken aback with its symbolism.

The gift was a cross of colored glass. Within the cross was a smaller cross and an engraved word. Linus was amazed and humbled with his gift. He immediately understood the significance and was grateful for the reminder. Linus believed that Jesus was telling him to carry the smaller crosses of life on earth, knowing the large cross was already taken care of by the suffering and death of Jesus.

The "bad hair day" was gone. Spending time with Ray's family gave Linus renewed faith and energy to carry on. The significance of the timing of our need for him, and the symbolism he feels in the gift will continue to provide him with a reminder of hope of depth after this life.

Amy was a gorgeous bride and everything was wonderful at the wedding. Linus and Craig did a great job together, and other than missing our Grandpa Ray, the wedding was perfect.

Being with Linus made us all feel a little bit closer to Dad. He was a joy to have in attendance at the family gathering. He felt better for being with those close to Raymond. We reminisced about the good times and some of Ray's best moments. Dad was very much present at Amy and David's celebration.

Heavenly Nurses

Dad was careful to give credit to his nurses during his illness. He would comment many times a day about his "heavenly nurses," and praise them for assisting him with love care.

One of the hospice nurses was apparently moved by the spirit within Ray's heart and soul. She was able to get to know Dad and was also present during the song and prayer sessions of the family.

This nurse let Mom know that she converted to Catholicism because of Dad. She felt a sense of peace while attending to Ray. He was ready to join his Savior and not afraid to die.

"Faith is unseen, but because of your Dad, we had sightings," was what Father had said about the experience with Dad's journey. I believe that these sightings encouraged many members of my family to revisit their faith, as well as inspire a few to seek God with more intent.

Brother Bear

"See through another's eyes, feel through another's heart, and discover the meaning of brotherhood."

Brother Bear is one of those movies that is funny and moving at the same time. By the time my nephew, Jack, sat through the whole movie, he had tears streaming down his face. His Mom asked him what was wrong and his answer was a very simple, "I miss Papa Ray."

Jack was a young boy when Papa Ray died. Jack knew him very well, even at three years old. Spending lots of time on the farm with Papa was an advantage Jack had over other grandkids that lived far away.

Although Papa was in his life only a few years, I believe Jack will be forever influenced by his grandfather. There are a few similarities that are difficult to miss. Both Papa and Jack have souls that are farmers through and through. A love of animals is shared between them. A cool rock is a gift to be treasured and kept in a special place. Laughter and a bit of Irish orneriness, reminiscent of Papa, can be seen easily by looking into the eyes of Jack.

Jack was so influenced at such a young age, enough so that a movie about a spirit moved him to tears. I take that as a sign that Papa, although in a different state, will forever be significant in our lives.

Mitch's Irish Tattoo

A very excited Mitch called me to share an idea to celebrate. It wasn't an expensive or extravagant gift he wanted. His idea made my heart soar with pride. As I've shared this with friends, they have expressed their thoughts on what a touching story this would make.

His idea was to go with me to a tattoo parlor and get matching Irish tattoos. Not only is the thought an honor because he chose to honor me by including me in his birthday celebration, but it's about Irishness, and that is my father in us.

The tattoo we are going to choose is an Irish symbol,

either a Celtic design or a small shamrock. Mitch's wish is to have "PAPA" engraved above the design. The idea of a nine-teen-year old boy wanting to engrave "Papa" on his body, with the symbol to represent his love for our wonderful little leprechaun, moved me to tears.

This story is simply a further reminder of how deeply Dad affected a variety of people. It didn't matter what age, what gender or religion. Papa Ray was an inspiration, a joy, and a messenger of hope and love.

A Few More Miracles

Dad suffering from this illness was a tragedy for my family. However, many good things came about because of it. All of us were checked for the same problems and many of us had a few minor things. My brother, Joe, had to have surgery, and the early intervention probably saved his life. The doctors told him if he'd have waited another five years to have a colonoscopy, it may have been too late.

Joe chose to talk about this at the rosary. Each of us spoke about something Dad said or had taught us. Joe told of Dad not discovering this disease until it was too late for him. He encouraged everyone in attendance to go get checked and to use Dad's experience to learn a lesson about early intervention.

Less than a month after the rosary, my mother received a letter of thanks from a friend that heard Joe speak that night. The following is an excerpt from that letter.

Dear Kay and family,

I just wanted to thank you.

. . . We'd heard Joe's story of his experience, and his request to others ("If you don't do it for yourself, do it for Ray"). So after Ray's funeral, we decided to go ahead and get the test for Dan.

. . . The doctor said, "I don't know what prompted you to come in have this done, but it was a very good thing that you did. Had he waited until he was 50, it would have been cancerous for sure. We feel very fortunate to have caught this before it could develop. I thank Ray and Joe for impacting me the way they did.

I hope all is well with you and your family. You will always be in my heart.

Thank you

Thanks, Dad. You've made all the difference in the world for many of us!

Chapter 29

Throughout the Journey: Humor

My uncle, Linus, calls Dad the king of the one-liners. Dad was in pain and barely hanging in there as far as we could tell. He wasn't eating anything and was sucking on a sponge to quench his thirst. But he still remained positive, faithful, and funny.

Dad had us hanging on his every word, and his delivery was amazing. Not only did he leave us with a renewed sense of faith and a deeper appreciation of family, but also with a new appreciation for using humor to enable us to get through **any** situation. Each time Dad would get tickled, he would cover his mouth with his hand and just giggle. It was the cutest thing in the world coming out of his frail little body. The following are some of the conversations that turned our stress into needed comic relief.

One of the first gatherings in his bedroom in a standing room only situation, I remember thinking, "Man, his sense of humor during times of sadness is truly unreal!" Dad, always a modest man, worrying that he was showing more leg than he wanted, was tugging on his sheet trying to cover up. Someone offered to help him and he quipped, "I don't wanna' show off my Paris legs. I don't want to tempt Sister Anna."

Sister chuckled and offered, "My greatest temptation."

Mom joined in, "I've been wondering what these two have spent all this time talking about back here."

Sister Anna had to leave after Sally died to be with Sally's family for awhile during their time of need. Before she left, she went into Dad to tell him goodbye. She thanked him for being the person he was, and stated her goodbye in a way that we all knew she thought it would be the last time she saw Dad alive.

Dad recognized the finality of this goodbye. As he lay helpless in the bed and to ease the tension a bit, he replied, **"I may have to sit down for this!"**

Dad's respect for Sister was immense. She went from helping us through Dad's illness to being with Sally's kids and helping them through their loss. Someone was commenting on her character, "Sister is a godsend."

From the bedroom, we heard Dad wholeheartedly agree, **"Darn tootin'!"**

Mom and Dad's bedroom during visiting hours lacked

enough seats for his audience. We would often scramble for a chair to allow more folks to pack in. One evening, we were at full capacity when Linus and my aunt Mary joined us. Dad had been too weak to get out of bed for at least a month by this time. Someone offered to go get Mary a chair, but she said she'd be okay on the floor. When she realized that really wasn't going to work either, someone else said, "I'll go get you a chair, Mary."

Dad, who was seemingly cognizant of everything, spoke up. **"I could get up and get you a chair, but God, I would hate to."**

At the time, we were amazed. He proved over and over again that he would remain very much himself during his final weeks, but for us it was difficult to know how that could be so.

Dad's love of Johnny Cash was discussed in many different ways. The trains that run through Frankfort all too often, the incredible way Dad could sing near the end of his life, the discussion of Ray singing even better than Johnny, etc.

During one of the bedroom gatherings–it may have been fear of missing his last words, it may have been hope of hearing some strength that wasn't going to come back–whatever it was, Dad KNEW we were all right there. He would share his wisdom. He shared his sightings of heaven, and then he'd set us up. **"I have something big to say . . ."** he began.

It was like the room shifted with everyone leaning in to hear. There was a perfect moment of hesitation on Dad's part, and then,**"I'm thankful I didn't call any of you boys Sue!"** The room exploded with laughter and the shaking of heads. He was ornery to the end.

A five gallon bucket became Dad's signature item. During times on the farm, the bucket would be full of grain for the cows, a cool rock for his collection, water for some tree he had planted, or maybe slop for the pigs. In the last months of his life, Dad called his trademark his "multi-purpose bucket." It was ALWAYS with him. There were times when he felt fine that he'd offer it to someone who needed a place to sit, as we were always short on chairs, but it was mostly a security for Dad.

Dad did not want to be caught getting sick without being able to take care of himself. He carried that bucket to the doctor's office, throughout the house, and wherever he needed to be–the bucket always followed. He started to comment on it as an explanation of its presence, but defended himself in the same manner. **"People may make fun of my bucket, but they need to respect the size of this bucket!"**

Many times in the last two weeks of Dad's life, we thought he had gone from us forever. One such incident found Mom trying to wake Dad up to talk to someone who had just arrived. Mom looked up and said, "I just don't think we are going to get him to rally this time."

Dad opened his eyes very slowly, turned his head to face Mom, and asked, **"Wanna bet?"**

Although Dad was very sick, he had stamina when it came to his family being with him. He was singing, praying, and alert! There were times when he would ask if WE needed a break, **"Anyone here need five?"**

"Do you mean a five minute break or a five dollar bill?" Mom asked.

"All three!" Dad came back in a very lively voice.

There were other times Dad would set us up, or wait carefully for the right moment for us to join in with his antics. Dad was preaching, once again from the packed bedroom setting, **"Consider us. WE are in heaven. Don't you think it should get to lookin' more like it?"**

"Yea," Bob answered, "I really thought it might be bigger!"

Another time, Mom suggested we break for a few minutes. Dad said no, we didn't need to. HE didn't need to use the restroom or anything. So, we kept prayin', singin', and visiting. It wasn't too long before John spoke up, "You may not need to urinate, Dad, but I do!" We took five.

Dad and Bob farmed together for many years. They knew one another very well and played off one another often. Bob is ornery, and Dad knew that. Dad was worried and shared that he thought he was stuck in purgatory. Bob said he figured he would spend a lot of time there himself. Dad said, **"I'm sure not going to argue that, Bob."**

Their interaction about heaven was similar. Dad was worried about why it was taking so long to die and get to heaven. Bob was trying to assure him and said, "Dad, they are 'prolly' getting your office ready."

Dad responded, **"I doubt they've even started working on yours yet."**

Amy and Stacey were missing one evening when we were gathered in the bedroom. Dad noticed and inquired. Bob told him they were making pizza for the masses. **"Masses. That is a good word,"** was Dad's quick pun. Not bad for someone on his deathbed, or so we thought.

My aunt and uncles and Mom and Dad used to travel together a lot. One summer, a group of them traveled to a rodeo in Cheyenne, WY. Dad discussed the need to find a "candy store" and went on the search. My aunt Mary thought they were truly looking for a store that sold chocolate, so kept quiet even though she was tired and ready to find a hotel.

Dad found a "candy store," but it was much different than Mary anticipated. It was a liquor store. Mary was exasperated and gave Dad a hard time.

She was still teasing Dad about the candy store the week before he died. As Mary was giving Dad a hard time about that trip, Dad's skinny arms lifted his tiny hand to his mouth and he giggled. What a testimony to love, laughter and life.

As Dad got closer to heaven, he sensed God's presence, but didn't let that take his humor away. One of the times he asked, **"Is God with us?"** He answered himself. **"Good. I'll try not to make any more wise cracks."**

I think God must have approved of his humor because his wise cracks and love of laughter lasted as long as he did. As Linus put it, "Ray never stopped being Ray."

Chapter 30

January, 2005: A Conversation with Father Bill

"**When I was with your Dad I FELT I WAS TRULY IN THE PRESENCE OF JESUS.** Ray would have suffered longer if he could have brought one more person to Jesus. That is what heroes are made of." I could tell that Father was ready to talk about his old friend Ray when I went to discuss my Dad with him.

Dad supported religious life. He had a huge amount of respect for anyone who chose to give his or her life to the Lord. Growing up, we all knew not to be in trouble with the priest. It would only mean double trouble at home.

Father Bill was an exception, because Dad supported him AND established a friendship that was unique. The bond between them was as close as family. Father expressed similar feelings. "Raymond was my friend. He provided me with a spiritual shower each time I saw him. I had a good cry when I found out he was dying. I'm always gonna miss him."

I told him I felt that Dad had accepted his illness and death exceptionally well, and the direction of this book was to illustrate that to others. He took off from there, and the hour and a half we had together flew by. Father talked freely and openly about the little Irishman of whom he'd grown so fond.

"Ray was so full of grace the whole time. After the surgery he had in October when the doctors opened him up and discovered the cancer had riddled his whole body, Raymond didn't deny; he accepted it with grace. I witnessed gentleness, a kindness to love life and all that there was. Your Dad had fear, but it was fear existing within his ability to die with strength and dignity.

When he realized there was not a miracle or treatment to cure his illness, he accepted it and wanted to continue to appreciate life with grace. To Dad it was basically this question. "Am I gonna' help the faith or hurt the faith? Will I do this with harshness or kindness?" Dad chose kindness. Ray most definitely helped the faith.

Father went on to explain that Ray was always more charitable to his neighbor and to others than to himself. Dad wanted folks to always look for the good in others. He took it very seriously to have everyone at peace. He would often pray that the world might know the love of Jesus. Ray understood that you don't bring people to love through hatred. He knew that the greatest sword is love.

"Raymond would pray for Muslims, for global peace, and he would pray for people in his daily life. Father relayed that he thought it was tough to pray for the people we meet everyday. These are the folks we may be jealous of, or we believe are petty. We know it in our minds, but it's tough to actually do–pray for those who hurt us. Raymond prayed for them anyway."

Father told me he was never too busy to talk to Dad. Ray would ask after daily mass, "Father, are you up for coffee?"

This question was posed frequently, and they began

to go almost daily. Father referred to the group that met to share coffee and a meal after mass as "The Breakfast Club with Jesus." Is there a better way to begin each day than breakfast with close friends and Jesus?

Father said he always looked forward to talking to Raymond. Dad's conversations never centered on himself. They were focused on others; he was never selfish. Talking with Dad helped Father to analyze that conversations should be around others. Dad helped Father to see what was truly important in life: relationships. Ray was always willing to point out the good in people.

I asked about Dad's influences in regard to Catholicism. Father shared that it was consistence through the family and not one specific moment. "Raymond was a cradle Catholic. Your grandma was devout, and the apple doesn't fall far from the tree. Your Dad got his mother's strength for forgiveness, because of your grandpa's drinking. He was also very self-conscious through the years about not falling into the same path."

"Faith was central in your Dad's life, but it was a balanced thing. Ray had the ability to see goodness and beauty. He could see through each of you kids without seeing your flaws. He loved each of you despite any flaws."

As Father spoke of Dad's love for his children, he told me that Dad understood how terribly wounded each of us were, especially on his deathbed. "Ray saw the good in every kid. He was very empathetic. Your Dad would suffer WITH each of you."

Dad's illness created an opportunity for an amazing transformation for the family. It was inspiring for Father to see the family, including all the kids, gathering together to help out.

Father added, "I have 15 nieces and nephews, and that is the best social security in the world. It's not money, not retirement, nothing tangible. It's family! I was reminded of that as I watched your family pull together to rebuild that house, to pull it all together for your Mom. That was your Dad's miracle."

"Your Dad was never afraid to talk about Jesus. His faith was ever-present; he lived it. He was very thoughtful and showed kindness towards folks who don't necessarily always get that. He wanted people to experience the faith and peace he had received from his faith. He wanted to give them someone to connect with."

"Another unique part of your Dad was that he loved to sing and he loved to hear people sing. I'll never forget walking into your Dad's bedroom with the whole family gathered around him. Raymond would ask for a song and you would all sing. I walked into Raymond praising the Lord; his skinny little arms reaching out to us-it was just like Christ on the cross, reaching out for us. Raymond suffered with joy. He gave others courage to suffer as well. Ray never stopped being Ray."

"When your Dad died, he served as an inspiration to Don Glen (a friend in the church) in his own death. Don was diagnosed with the same kind of cancer as Dad had, and was afraid of going through all that Dad had. Don was scared, but thought if my friend Ray could do this, I will do this too. Ray gave him faith and comfort. Knowing your father was affirming of both faith and marriage. Your Mom has tremendous beautiful strength. We experience God's love through people's presence. Although faith is unseen, we had sightings."

Dad being in heaven made it easier for Father when he was transferred. He feels Raymond is now with him all the time. Although he says it was still hard to leave Frankfort, Dad not being there made it a little less difficult for him.

Father shared what we both knew. Dad would have

tried to disagree with if he'd have been there to hear. He told me that Dad reminded him of two saints. The first was St. Thomas Aquinas. He was very intellectual and also saw glimpses of heaven prior to his death. Saint Theresa of Little Flower was the second saint Father saw in Dad. He said it was because Saint Theresa's ministry was one individual at a time. She reached many people by dealing one soul at a time.

"Ray may never be officially canonized in the Catholic Church, but I have no doubt that I have a saint in heaven praying for me. I'll call him St. Ray, the patron saint of friendly greeters, kindness, farmers, and loving fathers. St. Ray is in heaven praying for you and me. I know your Dad is in the communion of saints. He has a connection to Jesus. He loves me and the priesthood. God knows that is needed."

Chapter 31

Family Tributes

Evidence of Grandpa Ray's effect on so many of us was expressed in the need for many of us to write. My daughter, Addie, wrote this as an eighth grade student for an English assignment.

The Meadow by Addie Schroeder

I walked into my grandparents' newly remodeled townhouse. As I was just about to sit down on my Grandma's new couch, my Uncle John and Aunt Cindy walked out of the room with tears streaming down their faces. This was my family's cue to go visit with my sick Grandpa. One by one we filed into the room that smelled of disinfectant and illness.

My grandpa started mumbling about no one getting hurt on a trip to a beautiful meadow. Next, he said that he had found a trail in the midst of thousands of colorful wildflowers. The whole time he was talking, I was sitting in a rocker in the west side of the room by the doorway. My Mom was lying on the bed with Grandpa, and my brother and step-dad were sitting on trunks by the closet.

While my Grandpa described the flower-lined path, I finally realized that he was on the pathway to heaven. I realized that he had very little time left. Then it struck me: there was no hope. My Grandpa Ray was going to die. He was still talking about the meadow when I started sobbing and shaking uncontrollably.

On the edge of having to leave the room, Grandpa stopped giving his oration of the meadow. He kept asking, "God, are you here?" over and over again. We had figured out that he was not asking anyone on earth, but talking to God Himself. Next, Grandpa sang "Come Lord Jesus, Come" again and again. I finally stopped crying when it struck me that he was in too much pain to stay, no matter how badly he would be missed.

By this time everyone was quiet, for we were all listening to Grandpa's peaceful singing. I knew it wouldn't be long, but I also knew cancer was a very painful disease. I knew he wanted to join the heavenly banquet and get away from all the pain. Two days later my Grandpa died, and I knew he was in a better place.

My husband Craig has never been a man of many words. He tends to keep his emotions contained. However, his experience with Papa Ray inspired him to write this account.

My Husband's Account

Throughout what some may consider a short life, I have experienced many things. Some of those experiences helped to prepare me to assist in the care of Ray during the final days of what he referred to as his "earthly existence."

I have been a member of the Mitchell family since the latter stages of 1998, when I married Ray's youngest daughter. I can honestly say right from the beginning of my relationship with Ray, he was genuinely accepting of me and heartily welcomed me to his family. He maintained that spirit of acceptance right through to the very end of his earthly life.

The Mitchell family has always been very committed their Catholic faith. I'm not Catholic, so I've had the opportunity to "observe" their activities at their family gatherings from the outer fringes. This opportunity was very prominent many times during the last year of Ray's life. I was able to not only have an active role in, but also observe the transformations/changes not only Ray, but his family experienced during this time.

It was very important to Ray and his wife Kay that all the family be present for much of that final time. I have learned the Mitchell's are a very tight knit family, despite the size. Their definition of "family" is very much inclusive of a vast majority of the extended family, to include those well beyond the nuclear family, and is inclusive of all of both Ray's and Kay's siblings, children, grandchildren, etc.

My times with Ray during the final stages of his transformation were filled with all the extremes of emotions; from happiness, to sadness; to confusion, to apprehension; to finally the ultimate release. Ray's honest nature, dignity, pride, and commitment to his family never faltered. Perhaps the most amazing of his traits were his inner strength and his absolutely unfaltering faith.

Because of my medical training, I was able to take part in Ray's care when he became too weak to care for himself. It was very important to Ray and his family that he complete the final stages of his illness at home, surrounded by his family and friends. With the help of the local hospice nurses and several of the close family members, we were able to fulfill these wishes. I played a small role in his care along with my niece Amy, sister-in-law Janet, and Kay's sister, Sister Anna Marie.

Although very painful at times, this time offered me the opportunity to become more acquainted with Ray, as well as many of the of Mitchell and Broxterman family members on a much different level than had been possible up to this point. I am extremely grateful for those relationships that have truly blossomed as a result of our times with Ray. I truly believe this was one of Ray's goals during the final weeks of his life–to bring a family that in some ways had begun to drift apart back together. It worked. I am not the only beneficiary of those times. Many of the internal dynamics of the Mitchell family changed during this final year. Many hurts were mended, friendships changed, and developed.

I heard many stories and anecdotes from many different friends and family members as we all sat around Ray's bedside. I was able to participate in countless hours of sing-alongs, laughter, and many tearful goodbyes.

I have a fairly strong faith myself, although perhaps it is a bit different from most. In the final stages of Ray's existence with us here, not only his faith, but mine and many of the other family members' was at times tested. In his final days, it was apparent Ray was struggling physically. At times even he began to question why his physical existence continued. So did I. Though his questions were a part of Ray's final days, he really never faltered or lost sight of the ultimate goal. Ray's ultimate goal was to dwell in the house of the Lord and "dine at the heavenly banquet." He also made a point to insure there was room for all of us as well.

One of the stories I learned of during this experience concerned a "rope" dangling down from heaven one of Ray's sisters had "used" to get to heaven. He talked often of that rope during our times alone. Toward the very end, I reminded him often to hold on to that rope. Hold on to it, and use it to complete the final stage of the journey. I did quite a lot of listening during those times. I was asked, and readily assured him, I would do my part to make sure his family and his wife Kay were taken care of after his physical departure. Not once did Ray ever let the negative play into these final days.

During his final few days, we maintained a constant vigil with Ray. One of the four family members providing care for Ray was always there. These were some of the times I became most frustrated. Ray and the entire family were ready for him to complete his transformation from his earth bound life. During his final days, we all became sure he was truly moving between his existence here on earth and the forthcoming existence in Heaven with the Lord. During the last two to three days, it was increasingly difficult to tell if Ray was aware of us, but was apparent he was always seeking God. I became the same way—constantly seeking God and constantly questioning why Ray was having to continue facing things here.

Even though I wondered whether Ray knew I was there or not, he constantly wanted to hold someone's hand. It was during those times, when he and I were alone in his room, mostly late at night, I reminded him with as much strength as he and I could muster to "hold on to the rope."

The night Ray finally died, I was "off-duty" from the "late night shift" because my niece Amy was able to cover that night. I was lying awake in the bed at Diane's house because I knew, I hoped, things were finally drawing to a close. I had, along with several other family members, convinced my wife, Anna, to go home and get ready for the beginning of school. When the phone rang I knew what the call was. My first thoughts were of my wife. I knew she would not stay home and wait on me to come and get her.

One of my final acts of caring for Ray was completed that morning. After Dianne hollered down to me, I called Anna. I went back down to Kay and Ray's home. I made one more trip to that back bedroom, where a few of us waited for the arrival of the hospice nurse to make the final call and the mortuary to take Ray's body away.

Through my years with the emergency medical service in Abilene, and my years with the police department and sheriff's department, I had been present for this last of journeys for many different people. I had been there to assist with moving the bodies of many people to the cart to be wheeled away. I had helped to cover the bodies, and fastened the belts to hold them securely to the cart. None of those sheets seemed so final; none of those belts had that click, that final click as it locked into place. That is the hardest belt I have had to fasten up to now in my life.

I miss and always will miss Raymond Mitchell. He always had a kind word for me whenever I got to see him. He accepted me as family as if I always had a part there. He genuinely accepted me. My final words to him that fateful night were the same as they had been for several of the nights before then. "Hold on to that rope." I plan on holding on to it when the time comes, and will strongly encourage people I know to hold on to it when their time comes. I have no doubt who will be one of those at the other end of it when that time comes.

Epilogue

Months passed as I thought about the 'end' of this book. It was more than I could take to write my final thoughts of Dad. I decided there really never will be an end to his lessons or his influence. Perhaps the process of grief has taught me a huge lesson in acceptance. The loved ones we hold dear to us are never truly gone.

Souls of those we've been close to live on for many years and in many ways. There may never be scientific evidence of life beyond the grave, but I've lived through enough to **know** proof is not necessary.

In the state of grief in those last few weeks of Dad's life, I wrote him a poem. It was for him, for me, and for my family to grasp the idea that we weren't losing him. Fortunately, I was able to read this to Dad. It was one of those very difficult 'heart in your throat' moments. It was admitting he was leaving; it was accepting his death before he left. It was awful yet wonderful to share with him.

He's really not gone . . .
Anytime we strike up a conversation
With a complete stranger . . .
We'll realize Dad's not too far way.

Every time we bow our heads to pray
We'll know he's right here with us.
The next time we gather round a
Table to play cards, we'll feel his
Spirit in the high bids.

Giggles will erupt and hearty
Laughs will be shared. Compliments
Will fall from our lips with a greater
Frequency and we will find our hearts
More open and more forgiving.
No doubt Papa Ray is near.

Dad's humor, his love and respect, the
Kindness, the gentle nature, the gift of gab-
So many will continue hoping to be like him.

The sparkle in the eye of our favorite
Irishman will be carried on through each
Of us privileged enough to know the
Magical Lephrechaun, as Dad, Papa,
Grandpa or Ray. He's not gone.
He'll be in our heart for all of our days.
SAFE MILES, DAD. WE LOVE YOU. PASS IT ON.

After a brief silence in the 'standing room only'
bedroom, Dad shared a heartfelt **"Amen!"** His arms went
into the air as if leading a cheer. Tears were streaming down
many of our faces as we shared a tough bonding moment in

our lives. But Dad was smiling, his eyes sparkling, and we all were a bit closer to God.

It is interesting to read that poem now. I had a sense, but yet didn't 'get' it entirely. Dad would be able to show me how close he is, and how God is often tapping me on the shoulder, wanting to get my attention many more times since he died than I would have ever thought possible.

Sometimes Dad is with me in the form of a gentle breeze, in the Rays from the sun, and in the laughter of another's soul. With each of these occurs a soothing of my soul, and I know Dad is smiling. He is smiling with the knowledge that I've been touched by one of God's simple gestures.

There are other times Dad is so "right there." It's as if God places him amidst a regular day to remind me of what life is really about. We can easily move through our lives in a trance. Living becomes merely an act of getting through each day. Dad's ability to reach me through the daily grind is a blessing. His memory is a happy distraction. It sets me more right with the world again.

One instance occurred while I was teaching school. I currently teach Fifth Grade, and an expression I've never used before fell out of my mouth while praising one of my students. I witnessed a young lady being truly kind to one of her classmates. I reached out to put my arm around her shoulder and said, "Honey, you sure are a good egg!" I laughed out loud hearing my Dad's expression tumble out unexpectedly.

My student looked up at me with an inquisitive look. I explained, "I'm not sure if that was me or my Dad, but I'm thinking we both want you to know that was a really cool thing to do."

She beamed. Every student knows how I feel about Dad. Hearing that Dad and I both thought highly of her actions was an ultimate compliment. No one could receive higher praise from me.

Another time Dad's presence took me away from the normal stress of everyday life. Occasionally, I escape from the school day and go to grab a quick lunch with a friend. She teaches at another school in town and is released for lunch several minutes before I am, so she comes to pick me up. One of our lunch dates was much needed, as the day had been very stressful. I was more than ready to leave for a thirty-minute reprieve. I stood on the front steps of the school and was mesmerized by the bells playing at the church across the street.

The beautiful spring day surrounded me. The bells at the church across the street were playing "How Great Thou Art," and tears sprang forth from my eyes. The awareness of God's gifts to me were presented in a way that refused to be ignored. It was all there. Dad was more than gently nudging me to recognize the good in the world.

Although Craig and I sang "How Great Thou Art" without incident at Dad's funeral, neither of us have been able to listen to it since without tears and emotions overcoming us.

As my friend drove up, she witnessed my obvious emotion and asked what was upsetting me. My response was that Dad had been chatting with me, letting me know all that was right with the world. It had been a day of frustration and stress, but a few moments in the sun, with the right hymn providing background music, and I was able to see God's blessings. Dad comes through for me time and time again in ways I never would have believed before our experience through his death.

For each of us there are people and places that make us feel closer to Dad. My sister, Carol, has shared that our niece, Amy, is her 'people' connection, and the farm is her place to feel close to Dad. In my life, it's helping my husband with chores. It takes me back to the farm we grew up on and helping Dad do whatever it was for the day. Now if I'm watching the fence while he feeds the bison or making sandwiches while he and his pop build fence, I'm thinking of Dad.

My uncle, Linus, also brings him a bit closer. Linus has shared lots of stories with us about Dad since our summer of 2003. He is an extended part of the family in a more direct way than before. Dad's 'Cowboy Buddy,' with his guitar and bluegrass style, is more than welcome anytime any of us gather together.

Linus has the knack to make me question and explore my thoughts similar to the way Dad did. One of these instances was when Pope John Paul II died. Many of us discussed the opportunity Dad would have to talk with him in heaven. It was on everyone's minds that it was one of Dad's final wishes to change the world by talking with the Pope, Father Bill, and Sister Anna. Catholics and Protestants alike were commenting on how many days Dad would converse with the Pope before his thirst for knowledge from this leader was quenched.

I was privileged enough to spend some time with Linus and mentioned the conversation that surely ensued as the Pope found himself in heaven with Dad waiting for an audience. I posed the question of whether or not Dad and the Pope would now be able to 'make a difference' or 'change the world' now that Dad had his attention. Linus surprised me by responding that Dad already had.

He continued by sharing his thoughts with me. Linus perceives the way Dad died as a path for change. Dad accepted and suffered joyfully. He shared with us how to know Jesus as a best friend. Dad demonstrated the peace that comes from accepting Jesus as Savior and allowing Him to work in his life everyday. The fact that Dad's actions in his last two weeks of life were so adamantly FOR JESUS amazed all of us. Dad was suffering and could have easily been miserable and questioning God, or at least withdrawn and silent. Dad chose the high road WITH GOD. I know that he couldn't have done any of this on his own. Through Dad, God showed us FAITH.

Linus went on to say that each of us who were able to witness Dad in those final days were indeed changed. Denominations made no difference. Gender wasn't impor-tant. The size and shape of people had no impact. GOD was there. Dad shared with all.

The world would indeed be changed if we are able to follow through and be Christian day to day–IF we would all treat people in the same manner as Dad did in his time of ultimate distress. Regardless of the state of mind we were in, we would show others God no matter what was happening in their worlds, and life as we know it would certainly be different.

I appreciate his take on that and have pondered it many times. If we could each take Dad's lead and live as he did, the world would indeed be a changed place. We would each live forgiving one another and never judging. We would love as God intended, serving one another in spite of our own needs. If only we could become a little more like Jesus, our time on earth could be so much better.

There is no doubt in my mind that my Dad's influence upon my life will never cease. I try to implement his kindness and humor in my classroom each day. Dad also encourages me constantly in spirit. I have taught for a long time. Although I love children, I've wanted to explore other avenues. Dad used to say, "Anna, don't let security be your god." That certainly put a new spin on the commandment for me. I had always considered 'other gods' to be different faiths. . . . like Buddha or the Great Spirit. Dad opened up a whole new thought process for me with one phrase.

Another way Dad always encouraged me was by saying, "Use the gifts God gave you." He usually was prompting me to sing when he used this line. I feel that after his death, it was also about writing.

It's a scary venture to put your most precious memories on paper and offer them to others. I was fortunate to have God's hand on my shoulder throughout this experience. Doors opened, and I couldn't let the opportunity pass me by. Dad's story needed to be shared. His messages couldn't have been any clearer.

Dad's message to me was that death is certainly not the worst thing that can happen. He shed light on the entire experience. Accompanying him on part of his journey prompted me to think through many things and see them in a different way.

I'd always read the words to the 23rd Psalm, and

somehow didn't 'get' it in the same way as I do now. There are some personal ties to the words after Dad's experiences.

Psalm 23

> The LORD is my shepard, I shall not want.
> He makes me lie down in green pastures;
> he leads me beside still waters;
> he restores my soul.
> He leads me in right paths
> for his name's sake.
> Even though I walk through the valley of the
> shadow of death,
> I fear no evil for you are with me;
> your rod and your staff--
> they comfort me.
> You prepare a table before me
> in the presence of my enemies;
> you anoint my head with oil;
> my cup overflows.
> Surely goodness and mercy shall follow me
> all the days of my life,
> and I shall dwell in the house of the LORD forever.

For whatever reason, the 23rd Psalm had always been about a kind of scary place. I thought that in spite of the scariness, with the Lord, it would be okay. After Dad's journey, I look through this verse and see the multitude of positives within it.

Think of wanting nothing; would that be true peace? Imagine having the time and peace of mind to simply lie down in a green pasture. I so look forward to restoration of my soul, being led down the **right** paths after leading my own way down paths, praying and hoping to find my own way. No fear of evil leading me astray is another welcomed thought. The ultimate comfort: a table prepared, goodness and mercy all the days of life, and dwelling with the Lord forever. Sign me up! I don't know where I'd found the meaning earlier in my life but I'm so glad I have been enlightened.

I know Dad was ready for that table–the heavenly banquet. He is with the Lord. His soul is renewed and he knows goodness and mercy. How could I be sad????? Of course, I will always miss Dad, but I must see this in the very light he provided. I'm quite certain he shared as much as he could to lead us, and to be the beacon for his family to see the way.

God used Dad's death to affirm and strengthen my beliefs. I learned the difference between religion and faith. I gained an understanding of a 'heavenly father.'

I have no doubt Dad knows that I appreciate all that he went through to help me out. I **know** he hears my grateful heart saying, "Thanks, Dad. Thanks for the faith you demonstrated all through your life. Thanks for shining that light on the need for Jesus in my life. Your example lives in my heart daily. Your ways, your words, your favorite verses all have so much more meaning to me now. The last verse of your favorite Psalm resounds in my heart with faith renewed. . . ."

Wait for the LORD;
be strong; and let your heart take courage;
wait for the LORD!

I'm waiting, Dad. I'm anxiously waiting to join you at the banquet. I'm waiting to see the immense beauty you described. I'm ready to understand all of God's mysteries. Your death restored my faith. Your light in the shadow of death gave me hope, taught me how to hang on to family during times of stress, and demonstrated how to live with

Jesus as a friend to prepare for the kingdom of heaven."

If I can serve to be a light in the shadow of the darkness for anyone during the times of life's trials or tribulations, it will be a tribute to my dad. I will do my best to provide the light for those who are down and out, for the children who don't have all the love they need, for people of all ages who need a smile, a hug, or a shoulder to cry on. I can't be just like him–Dad's leprechaun ways cannot be duplicated–but I need to become a light in my own way.

The world could be a better place **now** if we could each search deep within our hearts and find the gifts God gave us to share. Sharing those gifts will provide a light for the world. If we all shine our light for those around us, the shadows will all be a little less scary.

Contact author Anna Zernickow
or order more copies of this book at

TATE PUBLISHING, LLC

127 East Trade Center Terrace
Mustang, Oklahoma 73064

(888) 361 - 9473

Tate Publishing, LLC

www.tatepublishing.com